D0115772

CAREER IDEAS
for kids who like
SPORTS

DIANE LINDSEY REEVES

Illustrations by
NANCY BOND

Facts On File, Inc.

CAREER IDEAS FOR KIDS WHO LIKE SPORTS

Checkmark Books
An imprint of Facts On File, Inc.
11 Penn Plaza
New York NY 10001

Library of Congress Cataloging-in-Publication Data

Reeves, Diane Lindsey, 1959–
    Sports / Diane Lindsey Reeves, illustrations by Nancy Bond
        p.   cm.—(Career ideas for kids who like)
    Includes bibliographical references (p.   ) and index.
    Summary: Discusses such sports-related careers as agent, coach,
fitness instructor, and sportscaster and discusses how to determine
which career might be suitable and how to prepare for it.
    ISBN 0-8160-3684-5 (hardcover).—ISBN 0-8160-3690-X (pbk.)
    1. Sports—Vocational guidance—United States—Juvenile literature.
[1. Sports—Vocational guidance.   2. Vocational guidance.]
I. Bond, Nancy, Ill.   II. Title.   III. Series: Reeves, Diane Lindsey, 1959–
Career ideas for kids who like.
GV734.R44   1998
796'.023'73—dc21   98-15203

You can find Facts On File on the World Wide Web at http://www.factsonfile.com

Text and cover design by Smart Graphics
Illustrations by Nancy Bond

This book is printed on acid-free paper.

Printed in the United States of America

MP FOF 10 9 8 7 6 5 4 3 2

(pbk)   10 9 8 7 6 5 4 3 2 1

In memory of W. Lee Reeves,
a wonderful father-in-law and
a man who ran a good race
in the game of life.

—Diane Reeves

ACKNOWLEDGMENTS

A million thanks to the people who took the time to share
their career stories and provide photos for this book:

Debbie Becker
Bob Beretta
Tommy Bowden
Julie Cook
Nancy Corbin
Richard DeLuca
Chad Foster
Joann Francis
Andy Johnson
Kevin Kahn
Jim Maurer
Dick Ratliff
Howard Rowe
Van Tate
Lionel Washington

Also, special thanks to the design team of Smart Graphics,
Nancy Bond, and Cathy Rincon for bringing the
Career Ideas for Kids series to life with their creative talent,
and to my resourceful research assistant,
Bethany Merz.

Finally, much appreciation and admiration is due to
my editor, Nicole Bowen, whose vision and attention
to detail increased the quality of this project in
many wonderful ways.

CONTENTS

MAKE A CHOICE!

You're young. Most of your life is still ahead of you. How are you supposed to know what you want to be when you grow up?

You're right: 10, 11, 12, 13, is a bit young to know exactly what and where and how you're going to do whatever it is you're going to do as an adult. But, it's the perfect time to start making some important discoveries about who you are, what you like to do, and what you do best. It's the ideal time to start thinking about what you *want* to do.

Make a choice! If you get a head start now, you may avoid setbacks and mistakes later on.

When it comes to picking a career, you've basically got two choices.

CHOICE A

Wait until you're in college to start figuring out what you want to do. Even then you still may not decide what's up your alley, so you graduate and jump from job to job still searching for something you really like.

Hey, it could work. It might be fun. Lots of (probably most) people do it this way.

The problem is that if you pick Choice A, you may end up settling for second best. You may miss out on a meaningful education, satisfying work, and the rewards of a focused and well-planned career.

You have another choice to consider.

CHOICE B

Start now figuring out your options and thinking about the things that are most important in your life's work: Serving others? Staying true to your values? Making lots of money? Enjoying your work? Your young years are the perfect time to mess around with different career ideas without messing up your life.

Reading this book is a great idea for kids who choose B. It's a first step toward choosing a career that matches your skills, interests, and lifetime goals. It will help you make a plan for tailoring your junior and high school years to fit your career dreams. To borrow a jingle from the U.S. Army—using this book is a way to discover how to "be all that you can be."

Ready for the challenge of Choice B? If so, read the next section to find out how this book can help start you on your way.

HOW TO USE THIS BOOK

This isn't a book about interesting careers that other people have. It's a book about interesting careers that you can have.

Of course, it won't do you a bit of good to just read this book. To get the whole shebang, you're going to have to jump in with both feet, roll up your sleeves, put on your thinking cap—whatever it takes—to help you do these three things:

☀ **Discover** what you do best and enjoy the most. (This is the secret ingredient for finding work that's perfect for you.)

☼ **Explore** ways to match your interests and abilities with career ideas.

☼ **Experiment** with lots of different ideas until you find the ideal career. (It's like trying on all kinds of hats to see which ones fit!)

Use this book as a road map to some exciting career destinations. Here's what to expect in the chapters that follow.

GET IN GEAR!

First stop: self-discovery. These activities will help you uncover important clues about the special traits and abilities that make you *you*. When you are finished you will have developed a personal Skill Set that will help guide you to career ideas in the next chapter.

TAKE A TRIP!

Next stop: exploration. Cruise down the career idea highway and find out about a variety of career ideas that are especially appropriate for people who like sports. Use the Skill Set chart at the beginning of each entry to match your own interests with those required for success on the job.

MAKE A SPORTY DETOUR!

Here's your chance to explore up-and-coming opportunities in athletics and fitness as well as the related fields of recreation, sports information, and athlete representation.

Just when you thought you'd seen it all, here come dozens of sports ideas to add to the career mix. Charge up your career search by learning all you can about some of these opportunities.

DON'T STOP NOW!

Third stop: experimentation. The library, the telephone, a computer, and a mentor—four keys to a successful career planning adventure. Use them well, and before long you'll be on the trail of some hot career ideas.

WHAT'S NEXT?

Make a plan! Chart your course (or at least the next stop) with these career planning road maps. Whether you're moving full steam ahead with a great idea or get slowed down at a yellow light of indecision, these road maps will keep you moving forward toward a great future.

Use a pencil—you're bound to make a detour or two along the way. But, hey, you've got to start somewhere.

HOORAY! YOU DID IT!

Some final rules of the road before sending you off to new adventures.

SOME FUTURE DESTINATIONS

This section lists a few career planning tools you'll want to know about.

You've got a lot of ground to cover in this phase of your career planning journey. Start your engines and get ready for an exciting adventure!

GET IN GEAR!

Career planning is a lifelong journey. There's usually more than one way to get where you're going, and there are often some interesting detours along the way. But, you have to start somewhere. So, rev up and find out all you can about you—one-of-a-kind, specially designed you. That's the first stop on what can be the most exciting trip of your life!

To get started, complete the two exercises described below.

WATCH FOR SIGNS ALONG THE WAY

Road signs help drivers figure out how to get where they want to go. They provide clues about direction, road conditions, and safety. Your career road signs will provide clues about who you are, what you like, and what you do best. These clues can help you decide where to look for the career ideas that are best for you.

Complete the following statements to make them true for you. There are no right or wrong answers. Jot down the response that describes you best. Your answers will provide important clues about career paths you should explore.

Please Note: If this book does not belong to you, write your responses on a separate sheet of paper.

On my last report card, I got the best grade in _____.

On my last report card, I got the worst grade in _____.

I am happiest when _____.

Something I can do for hours without getting bored is _____.

Something that bores me out of my mind is _____.

My favorite class is _____.

My least favorite class is _____.

The one thing I'd like to accomplish with my life is _____.

My favorite thing to do after school is _____.

My least favorite thing to do after school is _____.

Something I'm really good at is _____.

Something that is really tough for me to do is _____.

My favorite adult person is _____ because _____.

When I grow up _____.

The kinds of books I like to read are about _____.

The kinds of videos I like to watch are about _____.

GET SOME DIRECTION

It's easy to get lost when you don't have a good idea of where you want to go. This is especially true when you start thinking about what to do with the rest of your life. Unless you focus on where you want to go, you might get lost or even miss the exit. This second exercise will help you connect your own interests and abilities with a whole world of career opportunities.

Mark the activities that you enjoy doing or would enjoy doing if you had the chance. Be picky. Don't mark ideas that you wish you would do, mark only those that you would really do. For instance, if the idea of skydiving sounds appealing, but you'd never do it because you are terrified of heights, don't mark it.

Please Note: If this book does not belong to you, write your responses on a separate sheet of paper.

- ❏ 1. Rescue a cat stuck in a tree
- ❏ 2. Paint a mural on the cafeteria wall
- ❏ 3. Run for student council
- ❏ 4. Send e-mail to a "pen pal" in another state
- ❏ 5. Find out all there is to know about the American Revolution
- ❏ 6. Survey your classmates to find out what they do after school
- ❏ 7. Try out for the school play
- ❏ 8. Dissect a frog and identify the different organs
- ❏ 9. Play baseball, soccer, football, or _____ (fill in your favorite sport)

❏ 10. Talk on the phone to just about anyone who will talk back

❏ 11. Try foods from all over the world—Thailand, Poland, Japan, etc.

❏ 12. Write poems about things that are happening in your life

❏ 13. Create a really scary haunted house to take your friends through on Halloween

❏ 14. Bake a cake and decorate it for your best friend's birthday

❏ 15. Sell enough advertisements for the school yearbook to win a trip to Walt Disney World

❏ 16. Simulate an imaginary flight through space on your computer screen

❏ 17. Collect stamps, coins, baseball cards, or whatever and organize them into a fancy display

❏ 18. Build model airplanes, boats, doll houses, or anything from kits

❏ 19. Teach your friends a new dance routine

❏ 20. Watch the stars come out at night and see how many constellations you can find

❏ 21. Watch baseball, soccer, football, or _____ (fill in your favorite sport) on TV

❏ 22. Give a speech in front of the entire school

❏ 23. Plan the class field trip to Washington, D.C.

❏ 24. Read everything in sight, including the back of the cereal box

❏ 25. Figure out "who dunnit" in a mystery story

❏ 26. Make a poster announcing the school football game

❏ 27. Think up a new way to make the lunch line move faster and explain it to the cafeteria staff

❏ 28. Put together a multimedia show for a school assembly using music and lots of pictures and graphics

❏ 29. Visit historic landmarks like the Statue of Liberty and Civil War battlegrounds

❏ 30. Invest your allowance in the stock market and keep track of how it does

❏ 31. Go to the ballet or opera every time you get the chance

❏ 32. Do experiments with a chemistry set
❏ 33. Keep score at your sister's Little League game
❏ 34. Use lots of funny voices when reading stories to children
❏ 35. Ride on airplanes, trains, boats—anything that moves
❏ 36. Interview the new exchange student for an article in the school newspaper
❏ 37. Build your own treehouse
❏ 38. Visit an art museum and pick out your favorite painting
❏ 39. Play Monopoly® in an all-night championship challenge
❏ 40. Make a chart on the computer to show how much soda students buy from the school vending machines each week
❏ 41. Find out all you can about your family ancestors and make a family tree
❏ 42. Keep track of how much your team earns to buy new uniforms
❏ 43. Play an instrument in the school band or orchestra
❏ 44. Put together a 1,000-piece puzzle
❏ 45. Write stories about sports for the school newspaper
❏ 46. Listen to other people talk about their problems
❏ 47. Imagine yourself in exotic places

❏ 48. Hang around bookstores and libraries

❏ 49. Play harmless practical jokes on April Fools' Day

❏ 50. Take photographs at the school talent show

❏ 51. Make money by setting up your own business—paper route, lemonade stand, etc.

❏ 52. Create an imaginary city using a computer

❏ 53. Look for Native American artifacts and arrowheads

❏ 54. Do 3-D puzzles

❏ 55. Keep track of the top 10 songs of the week

❏ 56. Train your dog to do tricks

❏ 57. Make play-by-play announcements at the school football game

❏ 58. Answer the phones during a telethon to raise money for orphans

❏ 59. Be an exchange student in another country

❏ 60. Write down all your secret thoughts and favorite sayings in a journal

❏ 61. Jump out of an airplane (with a parachute, of course)

❏ 62. Use a video camera to make your own movies

❏ 63. Get your friends together to help clean up your town after a hurricane

❏ 64. Spend your summer at a computer camp learning lots of new computer programs

❏ 65. Help your little brother or sister make ink out of blueberry juice

❏ 66. Build bridges, sky-scrapers, and other structures out of LEGO®s

❏ 67. Plan a concert in the park for little kids

❏ 68. Collect different kinds of rocks

❏ 69. Help plan a sports tournament

❏ 70. Be DJ for the school dance

❏ 71. Learn how to fly a plane or sail a boat

❏ 72. Write funny captions for pictures in the school year-book

❏ 73. Scuba dive to search for buried treasure

❏ 74. Sketch pictures of your friends

❏ 75. Pick out neat stuff to sell at the school store

❏ 76. Answer your classmates' questions about how to use the computer

❏ 77. Make a timeline showing important things that hap-pened during the year

❏ 78. Draw a map showing how to get to your house from school

❏ 79. Make up new words to your favorite songs

❏ 80. Take a hike and name the different kinds of trees, birds, or flowers

❏ 81. Referee intramural basketball games

❏ 82. Join the school debate team

❏ 83. Make a poster with postcards from all the places you went on your summer vacation

❏ 84. Write down stories that your grandparents tell you about when they were young

CALCULATE THE CLUES

Now is your chance to add it all up. Each of the 12 boxes on these pages contains an interest area that is common to both your world and the world of work. Follow these directions to discover your personal Skill Set:

1. Find all of the numbers that you checked on pages 9–13 in the boxes below and X them. Work your way all the way through number 84.
2. Go back and count the Xs marked for each interest area. Write that number in the space that says "total."
3. Find the interest area with the highest total and put a number one in the "Rank" blank of that box. Repeat this process for the next two highest scoring areas. Rank the second highest as number two and the third highest as number three.
4. If you have more than three strong areas, choose the three that are most important and interesting to you.

Remember: If this book does not belong to you, write your responses on a separate sheet of paper.

ADVENTURE

❑ 1
❑ 13
❑ 25
❑ 37
❑ 49
❑ 61
❑ 73
Total: _____
Rank: _____

ANIMALS & NATURE

❑ 2
❑ 14
❑ 26
❑ 38
❑ 50
❑ 62
❑ 74
Total: _____
Rank: _____

ART

❑ 3
❑ 15
❑ 27
❑ 39
❑ 51
❑ 63
❑ 75
Total: _____
Rank: _____

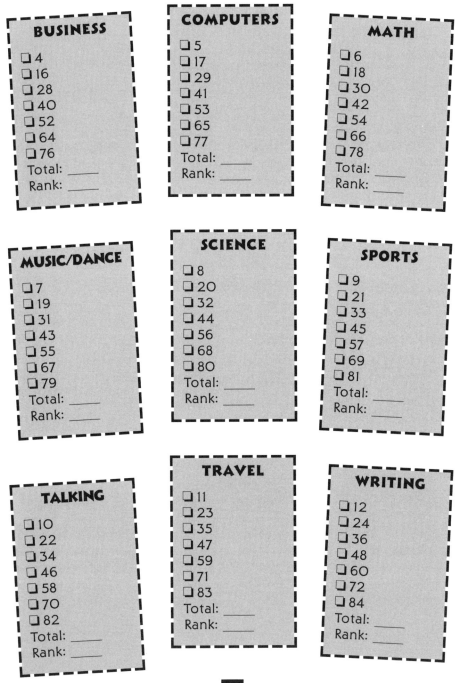

BUSINESS

- ❏ 4
- ❏ 16
- ❏ 28
- ❏ 40
- ❏ 52
- ❏ 64
- ❏ 76

Total: _____

Rank: _____

COMPUTERS

- ❏ 5
- ❏ 17
- ❏ 29
- ❏ 41
- ❏ 53
- ❏ 65
- ❏ 77

Total: _____

Rank: _____

MATH

- ❏ 6
- ❏ 18
- ❏ 30
- ❏ 42
- ❏ 54
- ❏ 66
- ❏ 78

Total: _____

Rank: _____

MUSIC/DANCE

- ❏ 7
- ❏ 19
- ❏ 31
- ❏ 43
- ❏ 55
- ❏ 67
- ❏ 79

Total: _____

Rank: _____

SCIENCE

- ❏ 8
- ❏ 20
- ❏ 32
- ❏ 44
- ❏ 56
- ❏ 68
- ❏ 80

Total: _____

Rank: _____

SPORTS

- ❏ 9
- ❏ 21
- ❏ 33
- ❏ 45
- ❏ 57
- ❏ 69
- ❏ 81

Total: _____

Rank: _____

TALKING

- ❏ 10
- ❏ 22
- ❏ 34
- ❏ 46
- ❏ 58
- ❏ 70
- ❏ 82

Total: _____

Rank: _____

TRAVEL

- ❏ 11
- ❏ 23
- ❏ 35
- ❏ 47
- ❏ 59
- ❏ 71
- ❏ 83

Total: _____

Rank: _____

WRITING

- ❏ 12
- ❏ 24
- ❏ 36
- ❏ 48
- ❏ 60
- ❏ 72
- ❏ 84

Total: _____

Rank: _____

What are your top three interest areas? List them here (or on a separate piece of paper).

1. _____

2. _____

3. _____

This is your personal *Skill Set* and provides important clues about the kinds of work you're most likely to enjoy. Remember it and look for career ideas with a skill set that matches yours most closely.

TAKE A TRIP!

Cruise down the
career idea highway
and enjoy in-depth pro-
files of some of the interesting options in this field. Keep in
mind all that you've discovered about yourself so far. Find
the careers that match your own Skill Set first. After that,
keep on trucking through the other ideas—exploration is
the name of this game.

If becoming a professional athlete is your dream and
you've got the talent, then go for it with all you've got. But
remember, playing sports is only one way to make a living in
the multibillion dollar sports industry. Make sure that you also
have a full understanding of all the exciting ways to build a

career around sports. Even those who do make it to the pros need to have a plan for life after their playing days are over.

The sports industry in the United States employs more than 4 million people. Only a small percentage of this number represents players. That means there's plenty of opportunity for an amazing variety of sports-related career options. So, hold fast to your dreams and enjoy this look at some of the many ways to make sports a big part of your career.

Meanwhile, as you read about the following careers, imagine yourself doing each job and ask yourself the following questions:

🔆 Would I like it?
🔆 Would I be good at it?
🔆 Is it the stuff my career dreams are made of?

If so, make a quick exit to explore what it involves, try it out, check it out, and get acquainted!

Buckle up and enjoy the trip!

A NOTE ON WEBSITES

Internet sites tend to move around the Web a bit. If you have trouble finding a particular site, use an Internet browser to find a specific website or type of information.

Agent

SKILL SET

✔ BUSINESS

✔ TALKING

✔ SPORTS

GO watch a professional sports team play and marvel at all the athletes you could be representing.

READ the *Business of Sports*, an on-line sports column by Andrew Brandt found at http://www.bizsports.com.

TRY getting involved in your school's peer mediation program.

WHAT IS AN AGENT?

Technically speaking, a sports agent is anyone who finds a good athlete, signs him or her as a client, and gets him or her a job with a professional sports team. Sometimes an athlete will ask a parent or trusted friend to serve as their official representative; however, the best (and most highly paid) agents tend to come from a business, accounting, or law background, and they often have strong ties to a particular sport. They represent a number of clients and are recognized as "official" agents by one or more of the professional sports organizations (NFL, NBA, etc.). Most important, they have earned a reputation for providing ethical and professional services for their athletic clients.

An agent's job is to negotiate the best possible contract for his or her clients. An agent serves as the go-between (and quite often, the voice of reason) between an athlete and the sports club. Sports agents must keep their client's best interests at heart while they work out the financial and legal details of a player's position with the team. In return, they receive a cut (usually about 5 percent) of the player's salary.

An agent's job isn't finished after a client is signed to a major team. An agent also looks for opportunities for clients to endorse products, appear in commercials, and make personal appearances. These sometimes lucrative opportunities can involve almost any product, from athletic equipment and clothes to hamburgers and tacos. An agent may also look for ways to involve a client in charitable causes and events. Sometimes agents also help their clients manage their finances and handle other personal matters so that the clients can concentrate on what they do best: sports.

Law, business, or accounting provide the necessary educational background to become an agent. To get on-the-job experience, aspiring agents would do well to start their careers in a sports management agency, a sports arena complex, a professional sports club, or any other place that involves working in the middle of all the sports action. Typical of any career where the financial stakes are high and the potential to earn big bucks is great, this is a very competitive profession. It takes a good business mind, a real love of sports, an ability to earn and keep the trust of clients, and a lot of hard work to find success as a sports agent.

TRY IT OUT

NEGOTIATE THE BIG ONE

It is safe to assume that the number-one financial issue fac-
ing most people your age is their allowance. Can you get by
on your current "salary"? Think about it and look for ways to
build a case for a raise. Have you recently taken on more
household chores? Maybe because of extracurricular activities you have more expenses like taking public transportation
or buying a snack to tide you over until dinner time. Come
up with a plan for negotiating an increase in your allowance.
Keep in mind the universal WIIFM (what's in it for me) aspect
of every deal and consider your parents' perspective. What
can you offer them in return for a raise? Pick a good time to
bring up the subject (such as when your room is clean and all
your chores are done) and pitch your plan. Next thing you
know you'll have to decide how to spend all that extra money.

BEEN THERE, DONE THAT

Learn the secrets of success from an agent who's spent more
than 20 years negotiating contracts for high-profile sports
professionals: Ron Simon shares it all in his book *The Game
Behind the Game: Negotiating in the Big Leagues* (Stillwater,
Minn.: Voyager Press, 1993).

Other books to read include *A Complete Guide to Sports
Agents* by Robert O'Connor (Madison, Wis.: Brown and
Benchmark, 1990) and *Minding Other People's Business* by
Donald Dell (New York: Random House, 1989).

WINNING WORDS

All successful sports agents are also successful negotiators.
Negotiation is a communication skill, one that involves thinking fast and accurately. It's a skill that can be learned. A good
way to learn the skill is by joining your school's debate team.
Through the team, you'll have the chance to look at both
sides of many issues, build a strong case for your point of
view, and present your argument in a public place. You'll

learn how to keep your cool under pressure and understand when it's best to keep quiet—skills an agent must put to use every day.

DRUMMING UP BUSINESS

Most agents actively seek their clients, rather than waiting for them to walk through their door. To snag the best clients, they have to keep track of new talent and be ready to approach them before the big offers start pouring in.

Get a head start on your career as a sports agent by learning how to spot tomorrow's superstars before they make it to the top. First, pick your favorite sport. Start following news coverage of high school and college players who seem to show exceptional athletic abilities. Make notes and keep news clippings about those you think might make it to the next level of being recruited for a good college or pro team. Keep tabs on their progress. Follow along for more than one season and see if your hunches are right.

CHECK IT OUT

Association of Representatives of Professional Athletes
1000 Santa Monica Boulevard, Suite 312
Century City, California 90067

National Sports Law Institute
1103 West Wisconsin Avenue
Milwaukee, Wisconsin 53233

Write to the following sports leagues to find out their rules for agents and to ask about internship opportunities.

Major League Baseball
350 Park Avenue, 17th Floor
New York, New York 10022

National Basketball Association
645 Fifth Avenue, 10th Floor
New York, New York 10022

National Football League
410 Park Avenue, 14th Floor
New York, New York 10022

National Hockey League
650 Fifth Avenue, 33rd Floor
New York, New York 10019

GET ACQUAINTED

Richard DeLuca, Sports Agent

CAREER PATH

CHILDHOOD ASPIRATION: To be a baseball or football player.

FIRST JOB: Working in a sporting goods store.

CURRENT JOB: President of Integrated Sports Management.

THE RIGHT PLACE AT THE RIGHT TIME

Sports has been part of Richard DeLuca's life from the time he was a child. In high school he focused on three sports: tennis, basketball, and soccer. At Tulane University, it turned out that his best connection to sports were his two athletic dorm mates. When they were offered contracts to play professional sports and were uncertain about a shady agent that wanted to handle the deal, they turned to DeLuca. They figured that since DeLuca was headed to law school he would know what to do.

DeLuca helped out his friends and simultaneously set the course for his career. He contacted a reputable sports agent and explained the situation. The agent said that if DeLuca could bring these new players to his firm, he would give DeLuca a job. That's how DeLuca wound up spending his first two years at law school at the University of Miami learning how to be a sports agent. When the agency wound up representing two first-round draft picks, things got so crazy at work that DeLuca left law school to devote all his time to his work.

Looking back, DeLuca credits three things for getting him where he is today: friendship, geography (the University of Miami had a number of top players back then), and his own desire to intermingle a career with sports and law.

MAKING IT WORK

Several years ago, DeLuca went out on his own and started a new agency. Knowing that he'd have to bring something substantial to the market in order to compete with other agents, he developed a full-service approach to player management. He had already learned that managing an athlete's finances was completely the opposite of managing the finances of other types of professions. Instead of starting out with low earnings and building to higher earnings over several decades, professional athletes start out with big earnings that drop drastically in very few years. DeLuca recognized that most athletes had just one shot at setting themselves up financially and had witnessed far too many situations in which the athletes make money early but then blow it, leaving them nothing when they retire.

DeLuca starts at the very beginning by identifying college football players with the potential to make it in the pros. Once his agency signs a player, the real work begins on two levels. One level involves aggressively "selling" the player to all the NFL teams with a well-orchestrated promotional blitz. On the other levels, DeLuca's firm works with the players to get them ready to survive in the business world. Sometimes this involves things as basic as teaching players how to balance a checkbook. Then the firm helps get the players established by setting up a bank account, securing a line of credit, and educating them about how to handle their finances.

Once an offer has been made and the all-important contract negotiated, more of DeLuca's full-service commitment comes into play. DeLuca's partner Tom Jacobs is an accountant, so he handles the financial side of things such as investments, taxes, and money management. DeLuca, meanwhile, makes it a point to touch base with every client at least once a week and travels to see each client play at least once a year. Some players feel as though DeLuca is part of the family.

FINDING A NICHE

DeLuca is keenly aware of the tough competition his firm faces in the sports industry. Through the years, he's learned to combat the situation by distinguishing his agency from the rest of the pack in unique ways. Certainly his reputation for taking good care of players and the full-service approach to player management are key to his success. Another point that sets his agency apart is that he and his partner focus on representing players from smaller colleges—schools that other agents tend to ignore.

The approach has obviously paid off since DeLuca's agency is one of the largest in the South and among the top 25 in the entire country. Representing players such as John Thierry of the Chicago Bears, Brad Maynard of the New York Giants, Reggie Barlow of the Jacksonville Jaguars, and Jerry Wilson of the Miami Dolphins, DeLuca has established himself as an agent to be trusted by players and reckoned with by other agents.

A DOSE OF REALITY

When young people ask him for advice about becoming a sports agent, DeLuca tells them, "don't do it." Of course he knows that for some people the pull of the profession is so great that there is no way that they won't do it. But he also knows the odds. For instance, while there are approximately 2,000 football players in the United States, there are about 1,500 agents (officially certified and otherwise). Since 10 of the biggest sports management firms represent about 500 players, that leaves 700 players for the rest.

If trying this profession is something you can't resist, DeLuca recommends starting with an established firm. He says that getting the first client is the toughest part. Get one, do a good job, and others will follow.

Athlete

SKILL SET

✔ ADVENTURE

✔ TRAVEL

✔ SPORTS

GO cruising on the Internet at http://www.prosports.com to learn more about a variety of professional sports.

READ *Sports Illustrated* magazine to keep tabs on your favorite players. Find it at the library, pick up a copy at a local newsstand, or request subscription information from *Sports Illustrated,* 1271 Avenue of the Americas, New York, New York, 10021.

TRY learning a new sport. You may discover talents that you never knew you had.

WHAT IS AN ATHLETE?

Just about anyone with a serious interest in sports has entertained thoughts of becoming a professional athlete. For some, it's a passing fancy. For others, it's a dream to be relentlessly pursued.

If you have hopes of someday becoming a great sports figure, the first thing you need to do is take a realistic look at what it requires. Media hype surrounding multimillion-dollar contracts and all the televised excitement of big game days may make the sports profession appear a bit rosier than it is for most people. Granted, sports can be an interesting and even glamorous way to make a living, but the reality is that it's not all fun and games. Before you set your heart on a career as a professional athlete, weigh the costs as described in the following "reality checks."

Reality check #1: Are you *exceptionally* good at your chosen sport? Notice the emphasis on the word "exceptionally." You may be the best player on your team or in your town, but do you have the talent to compete in a profession where there is fierce competition for each and every spot on each and every team? There's always going to be someone bigger and better than you. If you're going to make it in the pros, you have to distinguish yourself from the rest of the pack and show remarkable skill and staying power. Quite often, at least part of an athlete's success can be attributed to natural talent—you either have it or you don't. Other times success is as much a result of hard work and determination as it is of ability.

Reality check #2:   Are you willing to do whatever it takes to play your sport? There are some pretty high costs associated with playing sports professionally. Many of these costs can be summarized in one word: commitment. Playing at the top of any game requires a commitment to practice, practice, practice. That often means getting up earlier than everyone else and sticking with it when everyone else has gone home. It often means choosing practice over goofing off with friends, getting a part-time job, and other fun activities that are a normal part of a typical teenager's life. Commitment to the game doesn't start when you are on the payroll for a pro team. It starts right now and continues throughout your career. It boils down to choosing sports as the number-one priority in your life. Perhaps more than anything else, this decision to commit separates the wishful thinkers from those who have what it takes to go all the way.

Reality check #3: Do you want to play sports badly enough to sacrifice physical and personal comforts? It's almost inevitable that somewhere along the line a professional athlete is going to take a hard knock or two. Many athletes find that physical pain becomes a constant companion. Think about whether or not you want to risk your physical well-being for the sake of your sport.

When it comes to personal comforts, you'll also need to think about how you'd like spending a majority (or at least a good portion) of your time on the road. On one hand, a career in sports can be a great way to see the world. On the other hand, it can get lonely and boring being away from home, family, and friends so much of the time.

Reality check #4: Are you willing to start at the bottom and work your way up to the top? First, you'll have to prove yourself on the high school level so that a good college will pick you for the team. Then you'll have to prove yourself on the college level so that a pro team will even consider looking at you. Even after you've been signed to the big time, you may spend a lot of time playing for minor leagues or warming a bench waiting until you're ready to compete with the pros.

These are some real issues that you'll have to face if you're going to make it in this competitive profession. If you've thought through all these reality checks and are still game for a shot at the pros, here's what you need to do to move closer to making your dream come true.

Obviously, the first thing you need to do is play your sport whenever you can. Try out for the team and work hard to improve your skills. Record your progress on videotape. Once you play well enough, you can use some of the best action shots to put together a video résumé to send to coaches at colleges with notable sports programs. Ask your coach to help you choose colleges that match your abilities and aspirations. At the same time, make sure that sports isn't the only thing you work at while you are in school. Good grades are key to making and staying on any athletic team; if you flunk your courses, you're off the team.

Give yourself a chance at a lifetime of success and get a great education. Even in a best-case scenario in which you make it to the pinnacle of your sport, your career as an athlete will sustain you for only a dozen years or so. Be prepared to tackle the rest of your life with the gusto you brought to sports.

TRY IT OUT

LEAVE NO STONE UNTURNED

Everyone knows about the big three sports—baseball, football, and basketball—which means there's more competition to play these sports. Soccer and hockey are two increasingly popular sports with professional and semiprofessional playing opportunities. If you are convinced you want to pursue a career as an athlete, one of these sports may be just the ticket. Also, don't overlook opportunities to compete in some of the following sports:

automobile racing	ice skating	synchronized swimming
bodybuilding	lacrosse	tennis
bowling	racquetball	triathlon
golf	rodeo	waterskiing
gymnastics	skiing	weightlifting
horse racing	surfing	yachting

Before you rule out any of these sports, pick one or two that sound interesting, go to the library, and see what you can find out about them. One particularly interesting book that provides an overview together with plenty of fun facts and statistics is

The Guinness Book of Sports Records edited by Mark Young (Stamford, Conn.: Guinness Media, 1997). Another way you can find out more about each sport is to use an Internet web browser to run a search on your favorite sport.

KEEP YOUR EYES ON THE STARS

Every person who has ever excelled in sports started out just like you—with a hope and a dream. You can learn from other athletes' successes and failures. Pick a favorite sports hero or two. Start collecting all the information you can about his or her career and early background. You can find information in books, magazines, and newspapers. You can also use an Internet web browser such as Yahoo! or Explorer to find information on the World Wide Web. Compile everything you find in a notebook and keep tabs on your hero's career.

RAINY DAY SPORTS

Even the most dedicated sports players have to go home sometime. But, thanks to computer technology, the game doesn't have to stop. For nonstop action and some subtle athletic training tips, use your computer to play simulated sports games. You'll find quite a variety of options anywhere software is sold. Or check out the Front Page Sports games produced by Sierra On-Line. There are versions for baseball, football, basketball, golf, ski racing, and fishing. For more information visit Sierra On-Line's website at http://www.sierra.com or call 800-757-7707.

SHAPE UP!

Peak performance in any sport demands that an athlete be in top physical condition. Staying in good condition demands that you establish and maintain healthy habits in fitness and nutrition. Ask your physical education teacher or your coach to help draw up a plan for getting and staying in shape. Consider both nutrition and exercise. Make a chart to record your progress for a few weeks until these healthy habits become a part of your everyday lifestyle.

CHECK IT OUT

Amateur Athletic Union of the
United States
3400 West 86th Street
P.O. Box 68207
Indianapolis, Indiana 46268

Athletes in Action
4790 Irvine Boulevard,
Suite 105-325
Irvine, California 92711

Athletic Institute
200 Castlewood Drive
North Palm Beach, Florida
33408

Federation of Professional
Athletes
2021 L Street NW
Washington, D.C. 20036

International Center for
Athletic and Educational
Opportunities
P.O. Box 3113
Chicago, Illinois 60631

National Academy of Sports
220 East 63rd Street
New York, New York 10021

North American Youth Sport
Institute
4985 Oak Garden Drive
Kernersville, North Carolina
27284

Sports Foundation
Lake Center Plaza Building
1699 Wall Street
Mount Prospect, Illinois 60506

GET ACQUAINTED

Lionel Washington,
Professional Athlete

CAREER PATH

CHILDHOOD ASPIRATION: To
be a construction worker like
his dad.

FIRST JOB: Worked at a summer
camp for children.

CURRENT JOB: Cornerback for
the Los Angeles Raiders.

A NATURAL FIT

Lionel Washington first played football when he was 11 or 12 years old. He thought it was a fun game, but he played mostly because his friends were playing. He didn't play football again until he was in high school; instead he played basketball throughout junior high. Washington lettered in football, basketball, and track in high school, and it was about then that Washington started wondering if he just might be blessed with some natural athletic talent. Learning new sports came easy to him.

Playing the new sports well was another story. Washington was always keenly aware that there would always be someone out there who was better than he was. Knowing this motivated him to work extra hard. Even as a teenager, Washington set goals for himself and didn't let anyone stop him from reaching them.

All this hard work paid off when he received scholarship offers from colleges all over the country. He choose to stay close to his Louisiana home and went to Tulane University, where he majored in sports administration and physical education.

SOMETHING'S UP

Washington continued to excel at football at Tulane, but he also recognized that getting a good education was key to his future success. The academic part of college was very hard for him at first because he hadn't learned good study habits. He knuckled down and applied the same hard work principles that he used on the football field to his homework and was able to graduate in four years.

Ever since the summer he'd spent working at a camp, Washington had wanted to work with children, and he had every intention of graduating and getting a job as a coach. The NFL had other plans for Washington.

He was picked up by the St. Louis Cardinals in the fourth round of the 1983 NFL draft. He played with the Cardinals for four years until he was traded to the Los Angeles Raiders. As of the 1998 session, he'd been playing professional football for 15 years and held the record for playing the position of corner-back longer than any other professional in history. It's a tough position that requires as much mental strength as it does physical prowess.

MORE THAN MEETS THE EYE

Washington says that it's hard for most people to imagine how demanding it is to play professional football. The Sunday games are so exciting that it's easy to glamorize and over-simplify the situation. In reality, the players put in a lot of work between games. He discovered that using brain power is just as important as brawn when it comes to preparing for a game. Players have to review game films, read up on their opponents, and memorize complicated game plans. These guys have to stay on top of the game intellectually, and they are smarter than they are often given credit for.

OUCH!

Washington has been lucky enough to avoid major injury during his career. His recalls that one of his worst hits came from Steve Atwater, his own teammate. His whole left side went numb, and he thought for a minute that the gig was up. Fortunately, the problem was a temporary setback.

ADVICE TO ASPIRING ATHLETES

One word sums it up best: learn! Washington says that if you master the basics like reading and study skills, you won't have to struggle as hard to do whatever it is you want to do. Learn how to learn, and you can defeat any obstacle.

Also, don't put all your eggs in one basket. Washington urges anyone with a desire to become a professional athlete to prepare for it and pursue it with all you've got. Just don't let it keep you from considering other options.

Coach

WHAT IS A COACH?

Coaches are paid to win games. However, the actual coaching of games, the part that spectators see at sports events, is just a small part of a coach's overall job. Coaches have quite a few behind-the-scenes responsibilities. First, there is the job of picking the right mix of players with the hopes of turning the skills of many individuals into a winning team. This stage involves recruiting, observing, evaluating, and making tough decisions about who stays on the team and who gets cut. Once the team is created, they must get the players ready to play.

Coaches work with the players both on the field and off, helping them reach their personal best physically, mentally, and—in the case of high school and college coaches—academically. As teachers, they give instruction in the rules and regulations of the game. As trainers, they equip the athlete with skills necessary to compete in the game. As protectors, they do all they can to keep the players physically fit and free from injury. As motivators, they keep the team charged up and make sure that negative attitudes are kept at bay.

In addition to coaching teams in sports such as football, baseball, and basketball, some coaches specialize in individual sports such as tennis, golf, swimming, diving, figure skating, and gymnastics. Others may work as a private coach to just one athlete in preparation for a major sporting event, such as the Olympics or a world championship.

Perhaps even more than with other professions, athletic coaches must pay their dues. Nobody (repeat *nobody*) graduates from college and lands a first job as head coach of a professional sports team. Instead, one starts out on a high school or college level, and even there it's quite often as an assistant. At every level, the hours can be long and unpredictable, especially during the playing season. Overall, coaching can be an intense profession, since working with players and officials can be stressful.

With all that said, if you're still interested in becoming a coach, plan on going to college to earn a degree in a field such as physical education. You'll also want to make the most of every opportunity to play sports. If you can manage to land a spot on a college team, so much the better. If not, get involved in the sports program in any and every way that you can.

Coaching can be an exciting and satisfying career choice for sports fanatics who want to help other people succeed. It is important to have the inner strength to handle the team's victories as well as its losses.

TRY IT OUT

WEEKEND SPORTS MARATHON

Finish your chores, do your homework, and negotiate with the rest of the family to keep the television tuned to sports programs for the day. See how many different teams and how many different sports you can squeeze into a sports marathon. Use the remote control to bounce around to various events. Keep a list of each team and the outcome of each game. Also make a note of the name of each team's head coach and any details you notice about his or her coaching style.

ON-LINE COACHING

There is a wide variety of Internet resources that you can tap into to find out more about the coaching profession. One way to do this is to run a search using a web browser. Simply type in words that describe what you are looking for, such as *coaching* or *basketball coaches* or *Detroit Tigers* and see what you come up with. Here are a few specific sites to visit as well.

- ☼ Coaches Corner sponsored by the National High School Baseball Coaches Association is at http//www.baseball-coaches.org/.
- ☼ Gatorade Sports Science Institute at http://www.gssi-web.com offers information about topics such as sports nutrition, coaching and motivation techniques, and injury prevention.
- ☼ Coaching Youth Sports, a site hosted by the coaching staff at Virginia Tech, can be found at http://www.chre.vt.edu/~/cys/ and contains plenty of useful information as well as links to other sports websites.
- ☼ National Alliance for Youth Sports at http://nays.org is full of tips for coaches working with athletes between the ages of 6 and 16.

KNOW THE RULES!

If you're going to coach at any level, you've got to know the rules. Ask your school coach or community sports association for copies of the official rule book for your favorite sport. Or find out how to order an inexpensive software version of the rules for most major sports from Coach's Edge at http://www.coachsedge.com. Whichever route you take, learn the rules backward and forward. It will make you a better coach later, and it will impress your fellow teammates now.

ARMCHAIR COACHING

Learn from the successes and failures of coaches who have been (or still are) where you want to be. If you have a favorite all-time coach, find out as much as you can about his or her work and personal values. You can do this on the Internet by using a web browser to look for information or articles about a particular coach, or you can look in the biography section of the library for books about a favorite coach. Michael Koehler's book *America's Greatest Coaches* (Champaign-Urbana, Ill.: Human Kinetics Publishers, 1990) is another good source of insight and inspiration.

A WINNING SEASON

Become the youngest NFL coach in history with a little help from your computer and a software program called Madden '98. This game lets you create your own team, plan the season's schedule, and call the plays that lead your team to victory! Look for it at most software or office supply stores, or get more information by calling Electronic Arts at 800-245-4525 or by visiting the company's website at http://www.ea.com.

CHECK IT OUT

American Football Coaches Association
7758 Wallace Road
Orlando, Florida 32819

National Association of Basketball Coaches
18 Orchard Avenue
Branford, Connecticut 06405

National High School Athletic Coaches Association
3423 East Silver Spring Boulevard, Suite 9
Ocala, Florida 32670

National High School Baseball Coaches Association
P.O. Box 12354
Omaha, Nebraska 68112-0354

National Youth Sports Coaches Association
2611 Old Okeecheobee Road
West Palm Beach, Florida 33409

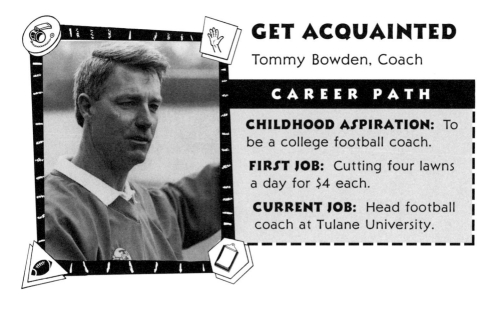

GET ACQUAINTED

Tommy Bowden, Coach

CAREER PATH

CHILDHOOD ASPIRATION: To be a college football coach.

FIRST JOB: Cutting four lawns a day for $4 each.

CURRENT JOB: Head football coach at Tulane University.

IT'S ALL IN THE FAMILY

Tommy Bowden is part of college football history. He is a member of the only family ever to have three college team coaches working at the same time. Tommy coaches at Tulane University, his brother Terry coaches at Auburn, and his father, Bobby, coaches at Florida State. He says it sure comes in handy to have all that expertise in the family when he needs some good football advice.

A GAME PLAN

Bowden says that he knew from the time he was very young that he wanted to be a college-level football coach. In fact, an autobiography that he wrote in the seventh grade lists coaching as his future occupation. Growing up around sports and having a successful coaching role model as a dad helped encourage the decision. But, he's always felt that coaching was exactly the work that he was meant to do.

This certainty provided the motivation he needed to prepare himself for the job—even though it required doing some things that he didn't really want to do. Bowden knew that if he was to reach his coaching goal, he would have to earn a college degree. So even though he really didn't like the idea of more school, he poured himself into his work and did what needed to be done. School was frustrating for Bowden because he didn't see what good classes in math and science and history would do him on the football field. Now he knows that one of the most important things that he learned in all those classes was the self-discipline to do something whether he wanted to do it or not.

Bowden says that since then he's had plenty of opportunities to put that self-discipline to work on the football field. Even in a job you love, there will be parts of it that aren't always fun. Football practice can be one of those things. Sometimes it's more work than play, but it's the only way to get ready for the game. He makes it a point to help his players learn this valuable life lesson too.

A LITTLE HELP FROM ABOVE

Bowden says that it can be a little scary having your future riding on how well a bunch of 18- and 19-year-olds play football. Any coach is considered only as good as his last season. If it was a winning season, the coach is considered great. If it was a losing season, the coach is generally out of a job. And if losing itself weren't bad enough, when you coach at the college level, every mistake you make is fair game for newspaper headlines and the television evening news.

Riding the peaks and valleys of coaching can get tough. Bowden says that his strong religious faith provides the stability and strength that his job sometimes lacks.

WHAT'S NEXT?

Bowden has had the opportunity to coach at several universities, including Auburn, Alabama, and Duke. The 1997 season was his first year as head coach at Tulane. Under his leadership, Tulane enjoyed its first winning season in 17 years. As satisfying as that is, Bowden is already looking forward to bringing the team even further along. He's shooting for a slot in the top 15 college teams and a bowl game or two. A chance at the national championship would be extra sweet!

ALWAYS HAVE A BACKUP PLAN

Although the young men he coaches bring many different kinds of skills to the game, there is one thing that they all have in common. Every single player on his team wants to become a professional football player. Bowden wouldn't pick someone for the team who didn't have that dream.

However, Bowden is keenly aware that only about 3 percent of all college players ever make it to the pros. That's why he encourages his players to have a contingency plan and tells them that a college degree is often the ticket they'll need to make the plan work. He tells them to "shoot for the moon, but if you miss, make sure you catch a star."

Facilities Manager

SKILL SET

✔ BUSINESS

✔ SPORTS

✔ TALKING

GO visit a sports arena or stadium and see if you can tell how well the facilities managers are doing their jobs.

READ *The One Minute Manager* by Kenneth Blanchard (New York: William Morrow, 1982). It's a classic about how good managers get their acts together.

TRY following your school's maintenance supervisor around for a while to find out how much is involved in keeping your school building in good working order.

WHAT IS A FACILITIES MANAGER?

It takes two teams to play many sports. One team, the athletes, plays on the field. The other team, the facilities managers, works behind the scenes handling the details that make serious athletic competition possible and enjoyable to watch. Long before the games begin, the facilities team is hard at work making sure that every aspect (and there are many) of running a sports facility is handled efficiently.

Facilities managers are the people who take care of all the details—everything from grooming the playing field to ordering enough food to keep the spectators happy. Facilities managers are sometimes hired by professional sport teams to manage sports arenas or stadiums. Other places where facilities managers work include golf courses, resorts, country clubs, colleges and universities, summer camps and retreats, and government-owned recreational properties.

The success of any sporting event—big or small, professional or amateur—is in the successful management of all these details. As with any business, there are several very specific areas that need the attention of skilled managers. One area is administration, where many of the day-to-day details of doing business are handled. Administrators are responsible for things such as personnel, purchasing supplies, and keeping tabs on other departments.

Other areas that need good managers include field maintenance, which is in charge of keeping the playing area in excellent condition; food service, which oversees the facility's concession stands and restaurants; and finance, where money matters such as payroll and budgets are handled. The operations department handles all the nitty-gritty details of keeping the building itself in good shape. Operations managers are basically responsible for keeping the facility clean and safe by monitoring electrical and plumbing services, security, and parking. Marketing, public relations, and sales managers are also part of the facility team. Another team member is the technical director whose main responsibility is managing all the audiovisual equipment that is needed for keeping score, broadcasting the game, and adding other creative touches that keep the audience informed.

As you can see, there is plenty of work to be done. The full-time management staff at a typical large sports complex con-

sists of anywhere from 10 to 25 people. Additional support staff may also work on a full-time basis. During a sport's season, thousands of part-time workers may be added to the staff to handle things such as serving food, parking cars, and selling tickets.

Although a college degree is not necessarily required, a degree in areas such as business administration, marketing, or accounting can provide a useful background and be helpful in reaching management level at a sports facility. Your résumé will stand out from the others if you've also had some experience working in a sports facility either as one of the seasonal hires or in some sort of support position. In many ways, running a sports facility is much like running any other business; however, there are enough differences to make on-the-job experience especially important for facilities managers. As a facilities manager, you may not play the sport itself, but you'll never miss a game!

TRY IT OUT

FOOD FOR FANS

One way to find out fast if you've got what it takes to manage anything is to volunteer to organize a refreshments stand for your school's sporting events. If your school already has a concession booth, this may be as easy as volunteering to help keep supplies stocked and run things during the games.

If this is a brand-new venture, you'll have a little more work to do. First, you'll have to decide on a menu. Simple, prepackaged snacks are probably the best bet: chips, candy, soda, and other kinds of goodies. Shop around to find the best prices on bulk purchases (discount price clubs, such as Sam's or Costco, might be a good place to start). At first, you'll have to guess about the kinds of things people will want and how much they'll buy. After a while, if you keep good records, you should be able to match supply with demand fairly accurately. Make sure to check with the proper authorities about rules and sales tax issues before you set up shop.

ON THE HOME FRONT

Whether you live in the suburbs, a big city, or a rural farm, your house is the perfect training ground for becoming a facility manager. Think of it as a small sports arena. Divide each of the various "departments" of your home life into categories on a big chart. Departments might include things such as food services (three meals a day), housekeeping (those weekly chores), maintenance (extras such as lawn care, trash removal, and repairs), and special events (appointments, sports activities, and other family happenings). Make a list of all the tasks in each department that are performed on a regular basis. Assign a manager to each department and see if you can come up with a plan for getting things done efficiently and with a minimum of fuss. Make sure teamwork is part of your plan, so include every family member in the plan. After you've had a chance to work out the details, present your plan at a family meeting.

SEE FOR YOURSELF

One of the best ways to find out if facilities management is a good choice for you is to work at a facility. That way you'll get an inside look at what it takes to make it work. Of course, you aren't quite ready to walk in and get hired as a manager yet. Instead, look for opportunities to work as a caddie at a golf course, a server at a stadium hot dog stand, or a groundskeeper for a recreation center. Do a good job and pay close attention to what your boss and your boss's boss do. That will give you a good idea of the types of things you'd have to do as a facility manager.

If you're too young to get an "official" part-time job, ask your school coach if you can lend a hand as a team manager. You may be assigned various tasks such as taking care of the equipment or keeping score at games. Take advantage of every opportunity to learn some responsibility and self-discipline, since both traits will serve you well in any career you eventually choose.

MANAGE THESE WEBSITES

Here are a few Internet websites that will give you a better idea of both the facilities and the management skills involved in sports facility management.

- ☀ Visit major stadiums around the world via the Stadium Manager's Association website at http://www.stadianet. com.
- ☀ Keep tabs on how various facilities prepare for big events such as the Olympics by visiting the International Association of Auditorium Managers website at www.scgt.oz.au.
- ☀ Learn more about the latest trends in management according to some of the leading experts in business management at http://w3.qualitydigest.com.

CHECK IT OUT

Athletic Equipment Managers Association
723 Keil Court
Bowling Green, Ohio 43402

Club Manager's Association
1753 King Street
Alexandria, Virginia 22314

International Association of Assembly Managers
4425 West Airport Freeway
Irving, Texas 75062

International League of Professional Baseball Clubs
P.O. Box 608
Grove City, Ohio 43123

National Sports Clubs Association
15 Tulipwood Drive
Commack, New York 11725

Stadium Managers Association
19 Mantua Road
Mt. Royal, New Jersey 08061

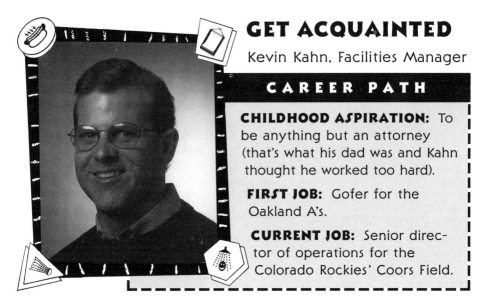

GET ACQUAINTED

Kevin Kahn, Facilities Manager

CAREER PATH

CHILDHOOD ASPIRATION: To be anything but an attorney (that's what his dad was and Kahn thought he worked too hard).

FIRST JOB: Gofer for the Oakland A's.

CURRENT JOB: Senior director of operations for the Colorado Rockies' Coors Field.

BEHIND THE SCENES

Kevin Kahn discovered a whole new dimension to the sports industry when in high school he was hired as a gofer for the Oakland A's. One of his teachers had told him that the Oakland A's had some jobs available and he jumped at the chance to get one. He soon found that a gofer does just that, go for this and go for that. His job was to do whatever his boss said needed to be done. For Kahn, that meant doing things such as delivering baseball schedules to sporting goods stores, handing out free hats on cap day, and all sorts of other jobs.

It also meant that he got a bird's-eye view of the entire operations division of a major league sports club. There he learned about the business side of sports and found a perfect fit for his own career ambitions. Kahn went to college to earn a degree in business administration with the goal of working in sports administration. In the meantime, he continued to work with the A's and was given more responsibilities. After he graduated (and his boss left for a job with another team), Kahn was promoted to facilities director for the A's. He later accepted a position with the Colorado Rockies because it gave him a chance to tackle new challenges in the Rockies' new, state-of-the-art, club-operated facility.

NO SUCH THING AS OFF-SEASON

As senior director of operations, Kahn heads the department that is responsible for security, parking, janitorial services, grounds and building maintenance, food and medical services, and guest relations. His full-time staff of 6 swells to about 2,500 employees on game days.

As busy as things get during the season, Kahn says it is even busier during the off-season. That is when he handles matters such as preparing the annual budget, recruiting and training game-day employees, publishing guest guides and employee handbooks, and making sure that everything is in tip-top shape. He manages maintenance crews as they paint, makes sure that all the bathroom fixtures and lights are in good repair, and gets everything ready so that the players and fans enjoy a fun day at the ballpark.

Of course, the hours tend to get longer during baseball season. Instead of the typical nine-to-five day at the office, the hours are more like nine in the morning until midnight.

FUN AND GAMES

Kahn admits that the biggest perk of his job is that all his friends think he has a glamorous job. While having an office at a 50,000-seat stadium is pretty unique, he says the work itself is not all that glamorous. Fortunately, he's happy to trade the glamour for the variety: For him, the best part of the job is that every day is different and full of new challenges. It's also fun to meet some of the famous people that come through the gates.

GET A FOOT IN THE DOOR

Kahn recommends that anyone interested in this side of the sports industry should consider applying for a game-day job or an internship at a sports facility. While there, he advises you to keep your eyes open and learn as much as you can about the various behind-the-scenes functions. Find out about the various departments such as promotions, finance, public relations, and operations to get a sense of where you might fit in. Who knows? You might get lucky and find your dream job, just like Kahn did.

Fitness Instructor

WHAT IS A FITNESS INSTRUCTOR?

The job of a fitness instructor is to teach and motivate others to get in shape and stay fit. It's fun work with a huge demand for well-qualified instructors. Fitness instructors enjoy the side benefit of keeping themselves fit while helping others stay in shape.

Fitness is in. Armed with plenty of research about the benefits that fitness brings to a person's health and productivity, the medical profession offers some of the best advertising that money can't buy and helps keep fitness instructors employed in all kinds of places. The fitness revolution is creating opportunities on several fronts, including health clubs, fitness centers and spas, corporate wellness centers, retirement homes and communities, and community recreation centers. While the programs may serve different types of clients, they all share the goal of making fitness and wellness a natural lifestyle choice.

Fitness instructors are primarily responsible for developing and conducting specific types of fitness classes. Classes may range from aerobics and water exercise to weight training or strengthening and conditioning classes. Fitness enthusiasts have come to expect well-planned and professionally executed classes, so fitness instructors have to know what they are doing and motivate their classes to keep up. They need to understand the relationship of various exercises to specific muscle groups and other "science-oriented" aspects of exercise as it relates to the cardiovascular system. They must enjoy working with all kinds of people and must possess energetic and sincere verbal communication skills.

Personal trainers, a particular kind of fitness expert, are becoming increasingly popular. Movie stars, professional athletes, and business executives were originally among the elite (and wealthier) group that could afford the luxury of having someone develop a highly personalized training plan and help clients implement the plan on a regular basis. Now, personal trainers are more widely available for a broader audience and are creating some interesting career paths for themselves. For instance, some may specialize in helping to rehabilitate injured or physically challenged people, while others may specialize in particular types of clients such as expectant mothers or traveling businesspeople. Personal trainers must complete specific training requirements and reach a higher level of certification than fitness instructors.

Other variations of fitness instruction include becoming a physical education teacher or a physical therapist. Physical education teachers work with students from the early elementary years all the way through college. A college degree and teaching certification are required.

Physical therapists work with patients who have limited use of their bodies due to injury, disease, or physical disabilities. Physical therapists must earn at least a bachelor's degree in physical therapy from an accredited college. Depending on a person's career goals, going on to earn a master's degree in rehabilitation therapy can be useful as well. Physical therapists work in hospitals and clinics, and some experienced, well-trained therapists may operate their own private practice offices.

TRY IT OUT

LIFESTYLES OF THE FIT AND HEALTHY

Effective fitness trainers have to stay current on the latest trends and findings. The Internet provides access to some of the most up-to-date information available anywhere. Visit the following sites and start flexing those thinking muscles.

- Balance Fitness on the Net at http://balance.net is an on-line magazine that covers topics such as exercise, health, diet, nutrition, sports, and injury.
- Find links to all kinds of exercise and physical fitness websites at http://www.selfgrowth.com/exercise.html.
- Health and Fitness Magazine at http://www.healthy-mag.com/www/bfit covers quite a few bases in the areas of health and fitness.

CREATE A HOME SPA

Everything you need to enjoy a personal version of a luxury health spa can be found at the local library. There you'll find books about general fitness and ideas for new exercise routines, exercise videos, and information about nutrition. Do some research and come up with a personal training plan guaranteed to help you get in shape.

You can also gain access to some of the best fitness instruction available anywhere via your television set. Check the local TV listings for various exercise and fitness programs. Try a variety until you find some favorites. Take note of what you like and don't like about each approach and be sure to integrate the good stuff into your own personal style.

THE OTHER SIDE OF THE COIN

Exercise is just half of a well-balanced fitness program. Nutrition is the other half. The Internet is a great source of informative, interactive, and even fun nutritional resources. Here are a few sites that provide food for thought.

- ☿ Gatorade's Sports Science Institute at http://www.gssi-web.com includes information about both training and sports nutrition.
- ☿ Diet Analysis at http://dawp.anet.com is a site where you can enter a list of the foods eaten on a given day, and it calculates the recommended daily allowances and lets you know how healthy it was.
- ☿ Fast Food Finder at http://www.olen.com/food is where junk food junkies can find the cold, hard facts about their dietary choices.
- ☿ Climb aboard Dole's Fitness Express at http://www/dole5aday.com for fun facts about making fruit and vegetables a part of your daily diet.
- ☿ The U.S. Department of Agriculture's Food and Nutrition Center provides all kind of information and links to other sites at http://www.nal.usda.gov/fnic/.

A LITTLE HELP FROM A CYBER FRIEND

Team up with your home computer to put together a personal fitness plan and use it to stay on track with your goals. There is quite a variety of products on the market including several that are reasonably priced. Browse through the health section of a software store or visit the website for Egghead software for a current list of selections. Egghead can be found at http://www.egghead.com, or call to talk with a customer service rep at 800-EGGHEAD. Two programs you may want to investigate are Active Trainer (from Lasar Media) and Total Body Fitness (from the Lifestyle Software Group).

CHECK IT OUT

Aerobics and Fitness Association
of America
15250 Venture Boulevard,
Suite 200
Sherman Oaks, California 91403

American Alliance for Physical
Education, Health, Recreation
and Dance
1900 Association Drive
Reston, Virginia 22091

American Association of Fitness
Directors in Business and
Industry
400 Sixth Avenue SW
Washington, D.C. 20201

American Physical Therapy
Association
1111 North Fairfax Street
Alexandria, Virginia 22314

Association for Fitness in
Business
956 Hope Street
Stamford, Connecticut 06907

International Association of
Fitness Professionals
6190 Cornerstone Court East,
Suite 204
San Diego, California 92121

International Sports Medicine
Association
P.O. Box 633
Richboro, Pennsylvania 18954

National Dance and Exercise
Instructor's Training
Association
1503 South Washington Avenue
Minneapolis, Minnesota 55454

GET ACQUAINTED

Julie Cook, Fitness Instructor

CAREER PATH

CHILDHOOD ASPIRATION: To be a teacher.

FIRST JOB: Worked at the counter at a fish and chips fast-food restaurant.

CURRENT JOB: Fitness consultant.

Photo courtesy of Frank Frost Photography

A LIFE-CHANGING EXPERIENCE

Fitness became a central part of Julie Cook's life after she'd given birth to her second child. Her weight had ballooned to 250 pounds and she found herself so heavy that she couldn't even bend over to tie her shoes. Fortunately, she was blessed with fitness-oriented grandparents. When she called them to cry about her weight-gain, they sent her a check to pay for her enrollment in a local fitness club. A trainer at the club took Cook under her wing and taught her that there was a lot more to losing weight and staying fit than eating salad and drinking water. The trainer recommended a plan including aerobics to burn fat and weight training to shape and trim her body.

The program (and Cook's commitment to stick with it) worked wonders! Her weight dropped to 130 pounds, and when one of the club's aerobics teachers moved on to another job, Cook discovered a new career. That's because the club asked her to start teaching her favorite aerobics class. It sounded easy enough, but Cook soon discovered that taking a class and teaching one were two completely different things.

However, Cook took this new opportunity as seriously as she had her goal to lose weight, so she started learning all she could. Another friend (and fan of Cook's success story) helped her get a job as a fitness instructor at a back rehabilitation clinic. The clinic offered to pay for her certification by the International Dance and Exercise Association and the American Aerobic and Fitness Association. Through this program, she learned about related areas such as exercise physiology, anatomy, safety, motivation, and principles of teaching.

She worked at the rehab clinic for a few years, eventually reaching the point where she needed a college degree to move forward in her career. Her certification training had sparked an interest in the scientific side of exercise and fitness, so she jumped at the chance to enroll in a new sports physiology program at a nearby community college. She got so involved in the program that the college asked her to sit on the board that developed a fitness technology certification program for the college.

THE FITNESS CHOICE

Cook's career in fitness has had several interesting twists and turns. She spent time working with senior citizens in a Fifty and Fit program. Many of this program's clients, faced with doctor's orders literally to do the program or die, had never exercised before and had to overcome their fear of working up a sweat. This experience was particularly enjoyable because the older students wanted to learn what she had to teach and really appreciated her help.

Cook has also worked in fitness clubs and spas, and she conducts private and semiprivate training sessions for a variety of clients. For many of them fitness is a preventive measure where they work out to enhance their quality of life and prevent serious disease such as heart attacks and strokes. For other clients, exercise is a means of recovering from injuries or other physical problems. It is a challenge to find just the right approach for each client's needs, but it's a challenge that Cook enjoys.

A REAL LIFESAVER

Cook is pleased with recent trends to encourage fitness at all ages. In a nation where it's estimated that 80 percent of people have back pain and heart disease is a number-one (and often preventable) killer, she believes her work can be a real lifesaver. Her own story is proof that shaping up your body is often the first step to shaping up your life.

Official

SKILL SET

✔ ADVENTURE

✔ TALKING

✔ SPORTS

GO watch various professional and amateur sports games and pay attention to how the officials call the game.

READ *Referee*, a magazine for game officials. Look for it at the library or write to the magazine at P.O. Box 161, Franksville, Wisconsin 53126 for subscription information.

TRY being an unofficial official. Call a game as you see it and notice how often your calls match the real official's calls.

WHAT IS AN OFFICIAL?

Sports officials are among the most important people at any sports field, arena, or rink. Known as an umpire in baseball and a referee in most other sports, a game official makes the calls on penalties, points, and other rules that ultimately help decide who wins or loses the game. The job demands that officials be "quick on their feet" mentally and physically.

Physically, officials have to be where the action is in order to call each play accurately. In some sports, this means that officials do quite a bit of moving from one end of the floor or field to another. Along with being physically fit, officials must be mentally sharp and sound. There's so much to absorb and process in any athletic event. Officials must be able to match the action in the game with the details in the rule book and make accurate decisions. They have to be confident enough in their judgment to stand by tough decisions even if it makes half of the audience angry. Focus, concentration, and split-second decisions are just part of the game for umpires and referees.

There's one more thing that no official should be without and that is a genuine love of sports. The job is intense and only someone who really respects the sports and the players can handle the heat on a long-term basis. The fact that officials are being paid to be somewhere that they want to be is probably one of the best perks of their jobs.

A college degree is not necessary to become a sports official. In fact, amateur officials who work for recreational or community teams may still be in high school. Many of these lower-level teams are almost always in dire need of officials, so there is plenty of opportunity to learn the basics. All it takes is a good understanding of the rules and a minimum investment in a uniform.

In order to officiate high school and higher level games, an official must be certified. Experience and competence are the two criteria that determine when an official is eligible to officiate at college level games. Those who have hopes of making it to professional sports should plan to attend special training programs or officiating classes (see training programs listed under Check It Out).

Most game officials do this type of work in addition to other jobs that allow them the flexibility to be available for game days and occasional travel to out-of-town games. Be prepared to start at the bottom and work your way to the top of this profession. Don't worry—it can be done. It just takes commitment and hard work to make it happen.

TRY IT OUT

SECOND-GUESSING

Make it a habit to pay attention to the officials whenever you watch professional sports on television. Whenever a call is made, see if you can guess what it is before the announcement. Keep a notebook handy to keep track of your success at second-guessing the officials.

PINT-SIZED OFFICIATING

If you like the sport and know the rules, chances are that there is a children's sports program that needs your help. Volunteer to help officiate games. Start with the younger kids' teams where the pace is slower and you'll have a chance to learn the ropes and work your way up from there. You have to start somewhere!

READY OR NOT

The work of a sports official can get very intense. As the ultimate authority on issues such as penalties and points, it's not unusual for an official to have lots of people yelling at him or her during a game. Before you decide to become a sports official, find out it you can take the heat. For starters ask your self the following questions:

- ☼ Do I like to compete and push myself past my comfort zone?
- ☼ Can I stay in control under pressure?
- ☼ Am I confident and able to project myself with assurance in front of a crowd?
- ☼ Do I think before I speak?

☼ Am I able to resist the urge to act like a tough guy when confronted by jerky behavior?

☼ Can I stay focused and avoid being distracted by noisy crowds?

☼ Am I willing to keep myself in good physical condition so that I can keep up with the action?

☼ Can I commit complex rules and regulations to memory so that I am able to make split-second decisions?

READ UP ON THE GAME

A must-read for all game officials is the rule book for the sport they observe. Get a copy from the team coach or the league association office. Learn the rules frontward, backward, and inside out.

Other books of interest to referees and umpires include

———————————

Baay, Dirk. *Blowing the Whistle: A Referee's View of Soccer.* Colorado Springs, Colo: Halftime Press, 1997.

Dirkson, Paul. *The Joy of Keeping Score.* San Diego, Calif.: Harcourt Brace, 1997.

Dolan, Edward. *Calling the Play: A Beginner's Guide to Amateur Sports Officiating.* New York: Simon and Schuster, 1984.

Dreimiller, David. *Sports Officiating Career Handbook: You Call the Shots.* Cleveland: Ohio: LR Publishing, 1997.

Gregg, Eric, and Marty Appel. *Working the Plate: The Eric Gregg Story.* New York: William Morrow, 1990.

McDonough, John. *Don't Hit Him, He's Dead.* Berkeley, Calif.: Celestial Arts, 1978.

Skipper, John C. *Umpires Classic Baseball Stories from the Men Who Made the Calls.* Jefferson, N.C.: McFarland, 1997.

———————————

CYBER STUFF

Pick a sport, any sport, and you are bound to find lots of information about it on the Internet. Use a web browser to introduce yourself to your chosen sport.

Some Internet sites of particular interest to sports officials include

- ☿ Amateur Baseball Umpire at http://www.superaje.com/ ~brenmcla
- ☿ The Last Word at http://sunsite.unc.edu/byers/ref/ index.html
- ☿ National Alliance for Youth Sports at http://www.nays.org
- ☿ Ref On Line at http://www.gmcgriff.com/refonline
- ☿ The Refeream Site at http://wwl.comteck.com/~jighm/ index. html
- ☿ The Referee/Umpire Home Page at http://www.sports-ref.com
- ☿ Umpire Resource Center at http:www.umpire.org

CHECK IT OUT

Major League Umpires Association
1 Logan Square, Suite 1004
New York, New York 10016

National Association of Basketball Referees
475 Park Avenue South
New York, New York 10016

National Association of Sports Officials
2017 Lathrop Avenue
Racine, Wisconsin 53405

National Football League Officials Association
4307 Trouthaven Drive
Murraysville, Pennsylvania 15668

Following is a list of some training programs especially for sports officials:

Academy of Professional Umpiring
P.O. Box 1641664
Austin, Texas 78716

Blue Chip Officials Camp
2076 Minton Drive
Tempe, Arizona 85282

Harry Wendelsteadt School for Umpires
88 South Andrews Drive
Ormond Beach, Florida 32074

Joe Brinkman Umpire School
1021 Indian River Drive
Cocoa, Florida 32922

Mickey Owen Umpire School
Department NS85
Miller, Missouri 65707

Nationwide Baseball Referee Camp
4520 Jolyn Place
Atlanta, Georgia, 30342

Nationwide Basketball Referees Camp
3694 Rex Road
Rex, Georgia 30273

GET ACQUAINTED

Howard Roe, Sports Official

CAREER PATH

CHILDHOOD ASPIRATION: To be an FBI agent.

FIRST JOB: Bagging groceries in a supermarket.

CURRENT JOB: Manager of university relations and career center at Lockheed Martin Astronautics and recently retired National Football League referee crew chief.

GOING PLACES

Howard Roe talks with a lot of college students about what to expect in a career. One thing he tells them is to expect to change careers about three or four times before it's all said and done. This has certainly been true for Roe. Roe started his career as a teacher and also worked as a counselor and a principal before leaving the field of education for the banking profession. From banking, he went to the oil and gas industry, and he finally landed in the aerospace business. At least that's what he's done for his day jobs. Somehow Roe also managed to squeeze in another career as a sports official.

PAYING HIS DUES

Roe got his start as a sports official with the children's basketball and football teams in the city where he taught school. He went on to officiate high school and junior college games.

Somewhere along the line, Roe got hooked on officiating and applied for a spot with the Big Eight College Conference Association. He worked high-level college games for seven years before being snatched up by the National Football League (the professional associations scout officials just like the teams scout players). For 13 years, Roe worked his regular job from Monday through Friday, jumped on a plane Friday night or Saturday morning, and spent the weekend calling the shots for NFL games. During his tenure as an official, he officiated at 265 games including 2 pro bowl games, 13 play-off games, and the Hall of Fame Classic in Canton, Ohio.

Pulling double duty with two jobs was tough at times but worth it. Roe has had the chance to travel all over the country, worked with some wonderful people, and officiated some of the most exciting games in football. He tells his two daughters that the good things that happen in life are often the by-product of some sacrifice made along the way. There were times that the long hours and time away from home were hard for Roe. But he says that if he had it do all over again, he would, and that's a very good thing to be able to say about choices in life.

PICKING FAVORITES

Roe says that officials can't pick favorite teams. Just to avoid even the appearance of favoritism, the NFL won't assign an official to games where his home team is playing. Now that he's retired, though, it's a different story. . . .

SOMETHING FOR EVERYONE

With all his work with young people and with sports, Roe is convinced that the two are a good mix. He believes that sports help young people learn self-discipline and teamwork, and he is excited about all the opportunities to participate in various sports at the high school and college level. He thinks there's a place for everyone to excel. His philosophy on the issue (and on life in general, for that matter) is this: Work hard, and good things will inevitably happen.

Recreation Director

WHAT IS A RECREATION DIRECTOR?

It is every recreation director's job to make sure that people have fun. Recreation work falls into two distinct categories. One is community recreation programs, and the other is commercial recreation programs. On the community side, a recreation director may actually work in any number of settings to provide sporting events and leisure time activities on a community level. Community recreation directors may be employed by a city, a county, or even a special district. Some specialize in youth programs and may work with child care programs, while others work primarily with the elderly in retirement communities or nursing homes. Others are employed by the national park service in nonprofit or government-sponsored programs that aim to serve the public.

On the commercial side, recreation directors work for businesses whose main goal is to make money. Places where you are likely to find recreational managers would include resorts, hotels, campgrounds, amusement parks, travel agencies, and cruise ships. Obviously, the duties at these various types of enterprises would vary greatly, but the general idea is to provide entertaining and memorable leisure time activities for travelers and guests.

Whether community-based or commercial, recreation program directors are responsible for developing, scheduling, and implementing various activities. In programs that cater to a variety of age groups, this can be quite a challenge. Activities may range from swimming classes for children of all ages and ability levels to gourmet cooking classes and square dancing classes for adults. A program director must be well acquainted with the needs of the various groups being served by the program and design a schedule of activities that appeals to each group. Successful program directors possess creativity, high energy levels, and a genuine interest in working closely with others.

Some recreation directors specialize in program administration and are responsible for handling the business side of programs. Their duties might include things like budgeting, marketing, and personnel management. Program administrators should be detail oriented, well organized, and diplomatic. Those with an interest in sports and other leisure time activities will find greater enjoyment in working in this type of environment than those who don't.

Additional recreational jobs include therapeutic recreational specialists who provide therapy treatments to help people recover from or adjust to illness, disability, or new social situations. Activity specialists are the people who implement recreational activities and provide instruction in special areas such as art, drama, music, dance, and sports.

There are a number of ways to work yourself into a career as a recreation director. Depending on your goals, you might pursue a two-year associate's degree in parks and recreation or a four-year bachelor's degree in recreation or leisure studies. Of course, it would be wise to get some experience in recreation before making a commitment to college. Opportunities abound for part-time program assistants and interns especially during the busy summer months.

There aren't many jobs that pay you to have fun, so this is one to think about if you are a fun-loving, physically active sports fan.

TRY IT OUT

BACKYARD OLYMPICS

Chances are that on a given summer day in your neighborhood there are at least a few children who have nothing to do. Ask your parents if it is all right if you organize a neighborhood version of the Olympics. Plan an assortment of relays and other tests of athletic prowess. Pass out flyers to the neighborhood announcing the time and place. Make sure to prepare a schedule of events for the big day and have a great time directing your first recreational program.

HOW DO YOU SPELL FUN?

A group of senior citizens probably have a completely different idea about how they want to use their leisure time than a group of preschoolers. Make a chart listing the following types of recreational scenarios. Leave lots of space in between and see how many different activities you can think of that might appeal to each group.

- 10-year-olds on a week-long cruise with their parents
- Older people living in a retirement community
- Business people at a convention
- Preschool children in a child care program while their parents work out at a health club
- A group of Japanese tourists visiting an amusement park
- Teenagers with too much time on their hands after school

FOR A GOOD TIME CALL . . .

Investigate what kinds of recreational services are available in your community. Make a list of all the programs you can think of and look for others in the phone book. Ask your local chamber of commerce to send a welcome packet—it's sure to be full of information about things to do in your community. You might also contact the city department of parks and recreation to see what options they offer. Once you've compiled a master list, look at it carefully to see if anything is missing. You might also want to use your new-found knowledge to enroll in a program to learn a new skill or sport. Keep the list handy when it comes time to go hunting for a summer job.

CHECK IT OUT

American Alliance for Health, Physical Education, Recreation and Dance
30 Mystic Isle Way
Becket, Massachusetts 01233

American Association for Leisure and Recreation
1900 Association Drive
Reston, Virginia 22091

American Recreation Resource and Education Center
7399 North Shadeland Avenue, Suite 242
Indianapolis, Indiana 46250

American Therapeutic Recreation Association
P.O. Box 15215
Hattiesburg, Mississippi 39404

National Association for Sport and Physical Education
1900 Association Drive
Reston, Virginia 22091

National Employee Services and Recreation Association
2400 South Downing Avenue
Westchester, Illinois 60153

National Parks and Recreation Association
2775 South Quincy Street, Suite 300
Arlington, Virginia 22206-2204

GET ACQUAINTED

Nancy Corbin, Recreation
Director

CAREER PATH

CHILDHOOD ASPIRATION: To be a teacher and work with children.

FIRST JOB: Assistant manager of a community swimming pool.

CURRENT JOB: Manager of cruise staff youth programming for Royal Caribbean International.

AN ACCIDENTAL TOURIST

Nancy Corbin has wanted to be a teacher and work with children for as long as she can remember. She graduated from a teacher's college in northern Iowa with credentials to teach any grade from preschool to 12th as well as special education.

This required a heavy course load, so by the time she was finished with her education, she was ready for a little break. Instead of taking a full-time job in a classroom, she started substitute teaching. For a little diversion, she also started working with some friends in a catering business. She enjoyed cooking, planning elaborate menus, and working with some of Iowa's important people.

One of her clients had made plans to go on a cruise with a friend. When, at the last minute, the friend couldn't go, Corbin was invited to take her place. It turned out to be a delightful experience and a turning point in her life. It just so happened that Corbin never went anywhere without a résumé, so she left one with the Royal Caribbean human resources department. Three days later she had a job working for the cruise line. It was quite a change of pace from life in Iowa!

STARTING FROM SCRATCH

Corbin's job was to create an onboard program that would appeal to families traveling with children. At first, the program was little more than glorified baby-sitting for a handful of children on any given cruise. As interest grew, so did the program. Now it's not at all unusual to have as many as 300 children of all ages enrolled during a three- or four-day cruise.

Corbin's approach is to provide "edutainment"—fun activities that sneak a little learning into the process. Onboard recreational activities for children may range from finger painting and dress-up for three- to five-year-old "Aquanauts" to wacky relay races and bearded bingo for six- to eight-year-old "Explorers." Older children and teens are engaged in activities such as sports tournaments, onboard investigations, and disco nights. Since many of the cruises make stops at exotic and foreign lands, Corbin makes sure that her young travelers learn a little about each destination.

WHAT A WAY TO SEE THE WORLD

Corbin spent five years sailing the world to distant ports in places such as Alaska, the Caribbean, Bermuda, Asia, and

Europe. Now she works shoreside, managing the programs on 11 different ships. Even now she doesn't stay in one place for long, as she makes visits to places such as Sweden and France to help design the actual space that's devoted to youth programs on new ships.

YOU'VE GOT TO LOVE IT
Working aboard a cruise ship can be as demanding as it is fun. It's not unusual for staff to put in 10- to 14-hour days. However, for every five months they work, the staff gets five weeks off, which leaves plenty of time to travel and relax.

SO NICE TO BE NOTICED
Corbin has been pleased to learn that other people think as highly of the Adventure Ocean program as she does. An America Online survey of cruise "critics" determined that four Royal Caribbean ships were rated among the top 10 for having the best children's programs, and the Family Travel Network rated them as the number-one cruise line for family cruising.

Sports Attorney

WHAT IS A SPORTS ATTORNEY?

A sports attorney is a bona fide lawyer who specializes in issues related to sports. On first glance, it might seem as though there wouldn't be much connection between sports and law. But the sports industry is more complicated than it may look on game day.

First, sports is a multibillion-dollar industry, and big money means big legal issues. Sports tend to be played in facilities that are rather expensive to build and take care of. Then, there are the players' contracts as well as liability issues and tax issues. There are many ways to be sued and ample opportunity for all kinds of lawsuits. There are league rules, labor laws, employee regulations, and even the U.S. Constitution to contend with. In fact, sports law covers such a wide variety of legal issues that it's considered one of the most complex forms of law for an attorney to practice.

That's why the successful practice of sports law is reserved for first-class lawyers. It requires such a vast array of skills and knowledge that anyone other than a hard-working, trustworthy, and truly dedicated lawyer would be doomed to failure.

Opportunities for sports lawyers take many forms. While in some law firms sports law is just one of a number of legal specialties, there are a number of law firms that specialize in the practice of sports law, and some also provide player management services. Either type of firm may represent individual players, coaches, teams, or other sports entities. Individual lawyers may provide in-house legal counsel for major sports organizations such as the NFL, the NBA, the NCAA, and major league baseball. In-house counsel means that the lawyer is an employee of the organization, and the organization is the only client that the lawyer represents. Other lawyers may work for or represent equipment manufacturers, colleges, sports stadiums or arenas, or player unions.

Becoming a lawyer requires some very specific and very demanding educational accomplishments. First, you have to earn a bachelor's degree, which generally takes four years of college. It doesn't necessarily matter what you major in although history, political science, English, and other majors with an emphasis on heavy reading and writing are good preparation for law school. No matter what your major, your grades are all-important. Getting accepted by a law school is very competitive, so only those with the best grades and the top credentials make the cut. After graduating from college,

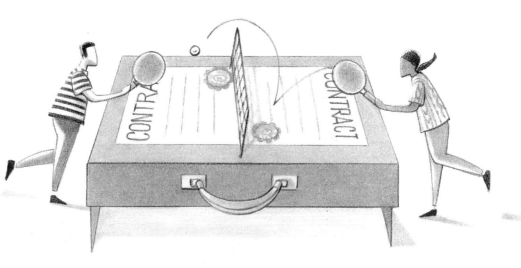

approximately three years of law school follow. Summers are often spent gaining on-the-job experience as interns in various types of law offices. The final step to becoming a lawyer is passing a bar exam. The bar exam includes a rigorous two-day written test and, in some states, an oral exam.

The idea of blending the glamour and excitement of sports with the practice of law is very appealing to quite a few lawyers, making this type of law a bit tougher to break into than other forms of law. It helps to have contacts in the sports industry, a determination to succeed, and finely tuned skills to bring to the profession.

TRY IT OUT

BOTH SIDES OF THE STORY

Your school debate team is a great place to hone your verbal communication skills, your logical thinking abilities, your ability to think on your feet, and your capacity for completely understanding both sides of an issue while wholeheartedly endorsing a single point of view. All of these are invaluable skills for attorneys of all kinds. Sign up for the debate team now!

RUN FOR OFFICE

Student council is another way to get a jump start on your future career. There you'll learn something of the democratic process, how rules are made and enforced, and the consequences associated with breaking them. Since laws are just a fancier form of rules, involvement in student government can be a great introduction to the basic "tools" that any lawyer works with.

BREAK IT UP

The next time a couple of friends get in a fight, test your potential as a lawyer by negotiating an agreement. You'll want to get both sides of the story and collect all the facts before making any decisions about what to do. See if you can mediate an agreement where both sides come out as winners.

INTERNET CONNECTIONS

Following are some Internet sites where you'll find more information about the practice of sports law:

- ☼ Entertainment and Sports Lawyer, a website sponsored by the American Bar Association, is at http://www.abanet.org/forums/entsports/.
- ☼ Admit One Sports and Entertainment Law Home Page is full of helpful resources and links and can be found at http://home.ici.net/~shamrock/sports.htm.
- ☼ The Sports Review, a legal journal, is located at http://www.livesports.com/baysportsreview/.
- ☼ The Business of Sports, an on-line magazine and news source, is at http://bizsports.com.

CHECK IT OUT

American Bar Association
740 15th Street NW, Ninth Floor
Washington, D.C. 60005

American Bar Foundation
750 North Lake Shore Drive, Fourth Floor
Chicago, Illinois 60611

National Lawyers Guild
126 University Place
New York, New York 10003

National Sports Law Institute
1103 West Wisconsin Avenue
Milwaukee, Wisconsin 53233

Sports Lawyers Association
2017 Lathrop Avenue
Racine, Wisconsin 53405

GET ACQUAINTED

Joann Francis, Attorney

CAREER PATH

CHILDHOOD ASPIRATION: To be a teacher.

FIRST JOB: Working as a motel housekeeper the summer after eighth grade.

CURRENT JOB: Attorney-at-law and chair of the employment and labor practice group for Foster Pepper & Shefelman.

A ROUNDABOUT ROUTE

Joann Francis is the first to admit that she never expected to be where she is today. Her career has come together as a result of both random circumstances and careful planning. It all started when she graduated with a degree in communications from the University of Washington. She wanted to be a news reporter and had the notion that she could walk into any of Seattle's television stations and land a great job. Wrong! They all kindly but consistently told her that she'd have to get some experience at a smaller station before they'd even consider hiring her. The idea of relocating to a small town didn't appeal to Francis at all, but the idea of having an unemployed college graduate around the house didn't appeal to her parents either. They gave her two choices: to get a job or to go back to school.

She opted for school and applied to law school as a way of sorting out what she wanted to do. She toyed with the idea of becoming a sports agent but decided that she didn't have the contact with athletes necessary to get started. Upon graduation, she says she was a reluctant lawyer and wasn't really sure that she wanted to practice law. Instead, she got a job as a special assistant to the mayor of Seattle, turned her attention to political concerns and got married along the way. After several years in city government, she and her husband quit their jobs and took off to see the world. Their trek (and their money) lasted about a year.

Back to reality, Francis found a job with Seattle's mass transit system, METRO, and got her first taste of working on projects requiring major public funding. She also gained experience working on issues that involved women- and minority-owned business.

SETTING UP SHOP

With expertise in these two very distinct areas of law—public finance and employment and labor issues—Francis started her own law firm. Her work focused on finance and bond counsel for publicly funded projects such as stadiums, roads, bridges, and schools. Later, she and a colleague started a second business, a management consulting company that helped other businesses comply with the regulations imposed by government.

THE SPORTS CONNECTION

Having satisfied the entrepreneurial need to have her own business, when a trusted mentor invited Francis to join the prestigious firm of Foster Pepper & Shefelman, she agreed. This is when sports came into the picture for her. One of the firm's clients was Paul Allen, owner of the Seattle Seahawks. When he called needing some special training for staff at one of his companies, Francis' expertise fit the bill.

As it turns out, all the experience she gained in public finance and employment and labor issues have really fit the bill as her firm has continued representing the Seahawks. They handle matters such as securing public approval for building a sports stadium with tax money, designing and building a stadium, and running the Seahawks' operation.

A WOMAN IN A MAN'S WORLD

Not only is the sports profession predominantly made up of men, but so is the law profession. As a woman, Francis is breaking new ground for her gender. She says that in her personal experience the advantages far outweigh the disadvantages. She's found that it's easier for men to accept the idea that she's a good lawyer than it is for some of them to get used to the idea that she knows something about sports. Sometimes she surprises them by knowing more about the game than they do.

Her experience has taught her that regardless of gender or race, there is simply no substitute for hard work. She says that it's not always easy but that being good at what you do and earning respect for your expertise are factors that can carry anyone wherever he or she wants to go. Francis advises everyone to keep an open mind. Don't limit yourself because you never know where new opportunities might lead.

PERKS OF THE PROFESSION

One of the best parts of representing a professional sports team is that you always have access to some of the best seats in the house for the games! Francis finds it amazing that her career path didn't follow a straight line but led her right to where she wanted to be in the first place—in sports law.

Sportscaster

SKILL SET

✔ SPORTS

✔ TALKING

✔ WRITING

WHAT IS A SPORTSCASTER?

Sportscasters are the voices behind the sports. Part journalist, part entertainer, and part sports fanatic, sportscasters keep the rest of the world informed about all kinds of athletic endeavors by reporting sports news on television or radio broadcasts.

There are several different kinds of sportscasting careers. Some sportscasters work for local or national news stations, where they are generally responsible for covering local and or major sports events, developing feature stories about sports, and anchoring the sports report on daily news shows. Other sportscasters work in radio. Their job might involve providing regular updates on sports news or hosting a sports talk show that discusses various sports issues at length. Opportunities for sportscasters in both radio and television have increased in recent years as national interest in sports has grown by incredible proportions.

Another way to earn a living by talking about sports is as a public address announcer for games on a high school, college, or professional level. This job involves making periodic announcements about the game, keeping the audience informed about who does what, making general announcements, and giving previews of upcoming events. The announcer can play an important role in setting the tone for the game. If the announcer is having fun, chances are pretty good that the audience is too.

At the top of the line of sportscasters are the play-by-play announcers who provide commentary and analysis of the action for televised sports events. Good play-by-play announcers provide so much detail and enthusiastic description that listening to them is almost as good as being at the game yourself. Some of the best-known announcers nationally—people such as John Madden and Bob Costas—are just as famous as some of the athletes they report about.

While all types of sportscasting jobs require excellent written and verbal communication skills, there are some marked differences in the other skills that they require. For instance, a sportscaster reporting on a local news station generally has three or four minutes of airtime to fill with news and commentary. Though it can be a challenge to fit all the news into such a tight time frame, the sportscaster does have the luxury of planning ahead and working from carefully prepared scripts.

In contrast, sports announcers and those providing play-by-play accounts of games may need to fill two to four hours of game time with meaningful dialogue. Their job is to explain each play as it occurs and what it means to the rest of the game. Nothing is more irritating to listeners than hearing some announcer talking about nothing while trying to fill the time. To avoid running out of things to say, sports announcers spend a lot of time studying the game and the teams that they cover so that they have deep reserves of interesting information to share during the course of any telecast. The most successful announcers tend to be the most colorful as well and are always ready with a funny story or amusing anecdote about one of the players.

Another difference between sportscasters who report sports news and those who announce games is the range of sports that they cover. Television and radio news sportscasters tend to report on all kinds of sports and must have a good working knowledge of a wide range of sports. Public address and play-by-play announcers tend to specialize in just one sport and must become virtual experts in that particular sport.

As exciting as it can be to have one of the best seats in the house for important sports events, there is one small detail that makes this type of work especially difficult: the hours. Since sports is part of the entertainment industry and since most people are more likely to be looking to be entertained in the evening, during the weekend, and over the holidays, it makes sense that these times are when most of this work is done. On one hand, it cuts into time with family and friends; on the other hand, many sportscasters ultimately decide that if you've got to work it might as well be at a ballgame.

Obvious skill requirements for any type of sportscaster include an excellent speaking voice, a reasonably attractive appearance for those who appear on-camera, and strong writing skills. It is generally considered a plus (if not absolutely required) to have some experience playing a sport on the high school, college, or even professional level.

To become a sportscaster, you'll need a college degree in a field such as journalism or communications. Unless you are very lucky, you won't be replacing any of the big-name sportscasters on ESPN right out of college. Instead, plan on starting your career in a smaller market, where you'll get the chance to gain some experience, get some contacts, and prove yourself.

Also, if you are intrigued by the idea of sports broadcasting but can't see yourself working in front of the camera, consider working behind the camera as a photographer, sports director, producer, or broadcast technician.

TRY IT OUT

IT'S ALL ON TAPE
The next time you go to a sports event, take your tape recorder with you. Call the game into the recorder describing every play as it happens. When you get home, rewind the tape and listen to it. Make note of your strong points and your weaker ones. Repeat this process every time you get the chance. When you reach the point where things are starting to sound pretty good, play your best tape for your school's coach or athletic director and ask for a chance to call one of the games.

PROVE YOURSELF
Good sportscasters make sportscasting look so fun that you can forget there's a lot of hard work involved in the job. Make sure your decision to be (or not to be) a sportscaster is based on the facts. There are two important things that you need to find out about yourself before you head in this direction. The first is whether or not you are a good speaker. Take every speech class you can and get involved in the school debate team. The second is whether or not you are a good writer. Take every creative writing class that you can and get involved on the school newspaper or yearbook staff.

Remember that it takes lots of experience and practice before anyone becomes a good writer or speaker, but if you enjoy the process, continue to show promise, and still think you want a career in sportscasting, then go for it!

TURN ON AND TUNE IN

Writing about sports for newspapers and magazines (the print media) is much different from writing for television and radio (the broadcast media). One is meant to be seen with the eyes and the other is meant to be heard with the ears. See if you can learn to see and hear the differences.

For this activity you'll need access to a computer and a television set. First, tune in to CNN, a national 24-hour news channel and listen to their sports coverage. Listen carefully, and take notes about which games and players they cover.

Next go to CNN's Internet website at http://www.cnn.com. Read the written reports about each of the stories covered on television. Identify the main points in each article and check your notes to see which ones were covered on the telecast. Compare the similarities between a televised report and a written one.

READ ALL ABOUT IT

In our sports-crazy society, there is no shortage of coverage about sports. For starters, there are the daily newspaper and television news shows, both local and national. Then, there's the Internet, where you can find quick access to the latest news via sites such as http://www.espn.com, http://www.sportsillustrated.com, and http://www.usatoday.com. For a look at women's sports, you can visit http://www.cnnsi.com/womens or http://www.gogirlmag.com. All of these sites can provide excellent ways for aspiring sportscasters to learn about the profession. Make it a habit to stay in touch with a variety of sports news sources.

In addition, there are a number of good books that offer insight into the sportscasting profession itself. For starters try books such as:

Bender, Gary. *Call of the
Game: What Really Goes
on in the Broadcast
Booth.* Chicago: Bonus
Books, 1994.

Fornoff, Susan. *Lady in
the Locker Room.*
Champaign, Ill.:
Sagamore Publishing,
1993.

Garrison, Bruce, and Mark
Sabljak. *Sports
Reporting.* Aimes: Iowa
State University Press,
1993.

CHECK IT OUT

American Sportscasters
Association
5 Beekman Street
New York, New York 10038

National Association of
Broadcasters
1771 North Street NW
Washington, D.C. 20036

National Sportscasters and
Sportswriters Association
P.O. Drawer 559
Salisburg, North Carolina
28144

Sportscaster Camps of
America
P.O. Box 10205
Newport Beach, California
92658

GET ACQUAINTED

Van Tate, Sportscaster

CAREER PATH

CHILDHOOD ASPIRATION: To be a clown so that he could make people laugh.

FIRST JOB: Earning tips by helping older women carry groceries to their cars at a Chicago A&P.

CURRENT JOB: Sports reporter and anchor for KRQE-TV in Albuquerque, New Mexico.

A KNACK FOR NEWS

If Van Tate had been paying closer attention, he might have known a long time ago that broadcasting was what he was meant to do. He says that even as a young child he liked to pretend that he was a news anchor reporting on the latest news. His mother made a tape of one such "broadcast" when he was seven years old (and really surprised him by playing it for him after he'd started his career as a television reporter). He also confesses that as early as eight years old he spent almost as much time watching news programs as he did cartoons. When he was in the eighth grade, he wrote for the school newspaper and really enjoyed it. The clues were there all along; it just took a while to make the connection.

Nevertheless, things just seemed to fall together easily on their own. He went to the University of New Mexico as a business major but found all the business classes boring. He's not really sure why he switched over to journalism; it just seemed like the right thing to do at the time. As it turns out, it was an instinct that forged his future.

OFF TO A GOOD START

After graduating, Tate got a job as a photographer with a television station in Albuquerque. The job required him to videotape stories for news broadcasts. The experience, it turns out, taught him a whole new way of writing and reporting stories because he learned to look at each story from a "big picture" perspective. Instead of writing words to match the pictures, he got the pictures to tell the story, so the words just naturally followed.

He got the chance to start reporting when the Albuquerque station bought a new station in a smaller New Mexico market. He was hired to do some general news reporting for the new station and started doing some sports stories on his own. When someone finally used one for a broadcast, the news director liked what he saw and started using Tate's stories on a regular basis.

After a while Tate put together a résumé tape and sent copies out to other stations. The effort paid off when he was offered a sports job in Savannah, Georgia. After a year working in Georgia, the news director from a station in Austin, Texas, called one morning to offer him a job. He was considering the Texas job when the news director from his old station called later that same day to offer him a spot back in Albuquerque. Since Albuquerque is home and most of his family still lived there, it was pretty easy to decide which offer to take.

BACK ON THE HOME FRONT

One thing that all of Tate's early experience taught him was that he preferred sports reporting over news reporting. He realized this when a colleague at work called some footage he'd gotten about a boy drowning "awesome." Tate's take on the same footage was that it was heartbreaking and awful. He was appalled at the notion of so casually diminishing the human tragedy behind the story and decided to focus on reporting the positive, straightforward news more commonly associated with sports.

Now Tate enjoys chasing down interesting stories about sports and reporting the results on the evening news. Tate especially enjoys working on regular feature stories. One segment that they run every week is called *On the Road* for which he does special interest stories about the people and events behind the sports. A recent story was about a women's basketball team with two sets of twins on the roster. The lighthearted story focused on how confused the opponents got trying to figure out who they were supposed to be guarding. Stories like this let Tate have fun with his reporting and add some "good" news to all the unpleasant mainstream news.

IT ISN'T AS EASY AS IT LOOKS
An average sports feature story lasts somewhere between a minute and minute and a half of actual air time. While that doesn't sound like much, it can be quite a challenge getting those ministories ready for a television audience. The process generally starts with lots of phone calls to track down just the right story. Then Tate and the camera crew have to go on location to shoot. Depending on the road time, it generally takes an hour or two to conduct the interview and get the video. Next, Tate has to sit down and write the story. This can take anywhere from a half-hour to a couple of hours depending on the story (although Tate admits that he has learned to be pretty quick). The next step is editing the tape for the segment. Editing involves choosing the best video clips and adding the reporter's story to it, and the process typically takes at least another hour. Essentially, several hours of work are required for every minute of airtime.

Of course, when reporting on actual sporting events, this process gets condensed. Sometimes the crew races back to the station after a game finishes at 9:30 P.M. and has to have the story ready by the 10:20 P.M. sports spot.

LEAVE THE EGO OUT OF IT
Tate offers two bits of advice for aspiring sportscasters. First, make a point of learning every aspect of the business. He

says the more you learn, the more opportunity you'll have. If you can shoot tape, write stories, edit, and anchor, you'll always have a job.

Second, remember that humility is an asset, even in the hard-nosed world of journalism. Even if you make it big, always remember what it's like in the trenches and appreciate the hard work of the behind-the-scenes people that makes you look good.

Sports Equipment Manufacturer

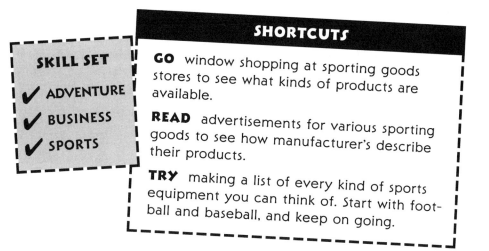

WHAT IS A SPORTS EQUIPMENT MANUFACTURER?

Baseball mitts, hockey pucks, and golf shoes—if you don't have the gear, you don't have the sport. The game can't go on without all the equipment, uniforms, and other paraphernalia that gives each sport its own identity. Sports equipment manufacturers make all those products, and they make lots of money in the process. These manufacturers come in all shapes and sizes, ranging from the sports-loving entrepreneur selling T-shirts at a game to the huge corporations that keep the world in running shoes.

If you want a career that keeps you connected with sports but doesn't require that you actually play a sport, the sports business may be just the ticket. To get an idea of the broad range of opportunities in the sports business, go watch any professional sports team play and make it a point to notice everything that is sold there: the drink cups with the team's logo printed on them, the game program, the uniforms the team is wearing, and much more. All those products don't magically

appear in the stadium or arena. Someone has to design them, find all the materials necessary to make them, produce them, package them, distribute them to stores, and sell them. Needless to say, that whole process provides plenty of opportunities for interesting careers.

Some of the easiest ways to break into the field are in the sales side of the business. You could manage a sporting goods store or sell a particular manufacturer's products as a manufacturer's representative. Both types of jobs will put you in touch with the products and the companies that make them, and either can be an effective starting point for a career in the sports business.

Another option that might appeal to sports fans who want to "be their own boss" is sports entrepreneurship. When it comes to sports, entrepreneurs run the gamut from the very wealthy businesspeople buying a sports team for franchise to the street vendors selling their products at a game. Entrepreneurs run businesses that publish sports-related information such as game programs and sports yearbooks, and they also run companies that provide services such as training programs. There is plenty of opportunity for creative sports lovers who have a good sense of how to run a business.

If the idea of working in a sports-related business appeals to you, think about the best way to mix your other strengths and interests with your love of sports. For instance, if you are a real math whiz, think about becoming an accountant and working for a company that makes sports equipment for a professional sports team. If you have strong communication skills, look at working in the marketing or public relations department for a favorite sports company. Professional career choices like these would require the same educational background as for any business: a college degree in accounting for aspiring accountants, a marketing or business degree for marketing specialists, a business degree for future business owners. If you want to work in a sports-related field but don't want to go to college, consider working in the production or packaging side of a manufacturing company, or look into the possibilities on the retail or wholesale side of things. There's something for everyone when you look for creative ways to indulge your passion for sports!

TRY IT OUT

MILLION-DOLLAR IDEA

Sometimes all it takes is a great idea, an entrepreneurial spirit, and lots of hard work to make it big in the business world. In the world of sports, those great ideas have included everything from producing snowboards and specially cushioned athletic shoes to manufacturing protective gear and sports training equipment. Think about a favorite sport and start brainstorming ideas for products that might make the game safer or more fun. Consider a particular sporting event such as a tournament or championship game and come up with ideas for T-shirts and other souvenirs.

To get the ideas flowing, you might want to look at the results of other people's bright ideas. You'll find an entire collection of unusual sports clothes and gear ideas at an on-line science museum exhibit. Take a tour from the comfort of your computer chair at http://www.nmsi.ac.uk/collections/themes/protective_clothing.html.

COMPETING FOR DOLLARS

There are many companies out there that are making a lot of sports-related products. And, as is true of any type of industry, competition is the name of the game. Usually, each company offers the same product but with a slightly different twist. As a sports player and customer, you have to compare all the different products and find the one that best meets your needs (and budget).

Pick a favorite sport and make a list of the gear you need to play it. Include appropriate sports apparel and the best type of shoes. Then the next time you go shopping, visit a couple of different stores that sell sports equipment. You may find a big discount store with a sporting goods department, one of the sporting goods chain stores, or a small shop that specializes in a particular sport such as soccer or skiing. Look for each of the items on your list and compare the prices, the quality, and the claims made by its manufacturer. Try to find at least two different brands for each item on your list. When you are finished, mark which products you think are the best.

SEE FOR YOURSELF

One surefire way to get an idea of the enormity of the sports business is to visit a trade show that exhibits a huge assortment of sports products. Two of the biggest and best are

- ☼ the National Sporting Goods Association World Sports Expo, held each year in Chicago. For information write the association at 1699 Wall Street, Mount Prospect, Illinois 60056.
- ☼ the Super Show, held by the Sport Goods Manufacturers Association in Atlanta. For more information contact the association at 1450 Northeast 23rd Street, North Miami, Florida 33161.

If it is not possible for you to visit one of these shows, write and ask for an event registration packet or program.

CYBERSHOPPING

You'll find information about sporting goods manufacturers and their products on the Internet. Read the labels on some of your favorite sports gear and use a search engine to find out all you can about the companies that make them. In addition, you may want to visit the websites of some of these big players in the sports business:

- http://www.addidas.com
- http://www.nike.com
- http://www.reebok.com

Another website you'll want to visit is http://www.cranbarry.com/. This interesting site tells the story of how hockey sticks are made. The story includes pictures that illustrate the entire process from beginning to end.

WORDS TO THE WISE

Find out the secrets of entrepreneurial success from someone who's been there. Chad Foster retired at the ripe old age of 33 after developing and marketing a soft, safe playground surface made from recycled tires. He shares that story as well his ideas on how young people can find their own brand of success in the book *Teenagers: Preparing for the Real World* (Lithonia, Ga.: Rising Books, 1995).

CHECK IT OUT

Association for Manufacturing Technology
7901 West Park Drive
McLean, Virginia 22102

Innovation and Entrepreneur Institute
University of Miami
Coral Gables, Florida 33124

National Association of Manufacturers
1331 Pennsylvania Avenue NW, Suite 1500
Washington, D.C. 20004

National Association of Sporting Goods Wholesalers
P.O. Box 11344
Chicago, Illinois 60611

National Sporting Goods Association
Lake Center Plaza Building
1699 Wall Street
Mount Prospect, Illinois 60056

Sporting Goods Manufacturers Association
200 Castlewood Drive
North Palm Beach, Florida 33048

GET ACQUAINTED

Chad Foster, Tennis Court and Playground Surface Manufacturer

CAREER PATH

CHILDHOOD ASPIRATION: To be a professional tennis player.

FIRST JOB: At age 13 he sold tennis shoes in a tennis shop where he learned more about business than with any other job he ever had.

CURRENT JOB: Author, ESPN TV host, motivational speaker, and retired playground surface manufacturer.

WHEN DREAMS DIE

Chad Foster learned how to play tennis when he was 13 years old. Tennis started out as a way to endure a miserable summer camp experience but ended up being a big part of his entire future. It turns out that tennis was Foster's game. He liked it, and he was good at it. As a teenager, he traveled all over the world playing on the junior tennis circuit. After graduating from high school, he went to Florida State University on a tennis scholarship. However, the professional tennis bug was just too strong to resist, and Foster dropped out of college to give his dream a shot. Things didn't quite work out the way that Foster had expected. After a year on the circuit with only $480 in winnings to show for it, Foster knew that he wasn't going to make it as a pro.

At that time, a man he'd met on the tennis circuit hired 19-year-old Foster to work in his tennis court surfacing business. All the people he'd met in his years on the tennis circuit now became potential clients. One of these clients also owned a couple of McDonald's restaurants and told Foster that he needed a safe surface for the playgrounds at his stores.

Foster did some homework and came up with an idea for a soft, safe playground surface made of recycled tire rubber. The resulting product, called SAF DEK, can be seen on thousands of McDonald's playgrounds around the world. It's also been used at the Walt Disney World and Universal Studios amusement parks. Needless to say, Foster found his fortune manufacturing and installing these playground surfaces. By the time he was 33 years old, he was able to retire and ready to pursue other things.

What did Foster learn in all this about chasing dreams? He tells young people that if they have a dream, pursue it, even if it is a long shot. If you don't make it, other doors will open along the way.

A FORMULA FOR SUCCESS

Based on his own experiences, Foster realized that he had learned some things about success that he never learned in school. He now devotes much of his time sharing his story with teenagers all over the United States.

Foster defines success as knowledge plus skills plus people. He says that it's not just what you know but who you know that will determine your success in life. In his book and speeches, he encourages students to meet people, stay in touch with them, and look for ways to help each other out along the way. Since Foster built a multimillion-dollar company with a contact he met at the age of 15, you can bet that Foster knows what he is talking about.

YOU JUST NEVER KNOW

Foster learned the importance of making and nurturing contacts from his dad. When his dad was a kid, he met a guy named Poppy. They stayed in touch by mail for more than 40 years, even though they never saw each other again. Foster's dad went to Louisiana and became a lawyer. Poppy, whose real name was George and whose last name was Bush, went to Washington, D.C., and became president of the United States.

Foster says that you never know. Meeting someone while working at your first part-time job flipping hamburgers could change your life.

GET PREPARED

Foster's book is full of great stories and fun advice, and it's one you'll want to read: *Teenagers: Preparing for the Real World* (Lithonia, Ga.: Rising Books, 1995). Find a copy at the library, buy one from the local bookstore, or order one directly from Foster's company at Rising Books, 3310 Waterford Way, Suite 100, Lithonia, Georgia 30058. You can also find out more about Foster's work at his Internet website at http://www.chadfoster.com.

Sports Event Coordinator

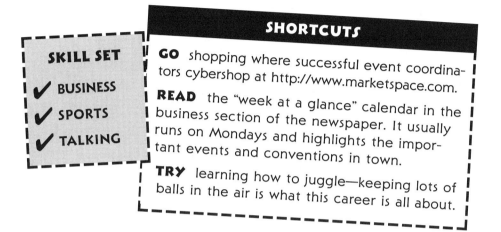

SKILL SET

✔ BUSINESS

✔ SPORTS

✔ TALKING

GO shopping where successful event coordinators cybershop at http://www.marketspace.com.

READ the "week at a glance" calendar in the business section of the newspaper. It usually runs on Mondays and highlights the important events and conventions in town.

TRY learning how to juggle—keeping lots of balls in the air is what this career is all about.

WHAT IS A SPORTS EVENT COORDINATOR?

Major sporting events such as the World Series, college bowl games, and the Final Four basketball championship don't just happen. There are hours, weeks, and sometimes even many months of intense planning and preparation that go into staging such events. Right in the middle of the planning process is a sports event coordinator. The coordinator's job isn't necessarily to *do* everything that needs to be done but to make sure that it *gets done.* In fact, a primary duty is to delegate tasks to other people and departments. Then it's a matter of keeping track of who's doing what and making sure that roles are clearly defined, that people know exactly what their responsibilities are, and that everything gets done correctly and on time.

If you've ever tried to get a group of friends together for a Saturday afternoon matinee, you may have experienced in a very small way what it's like to coordinate a sports event. Trying to get several people to the same place at the same time can require some fancy footwork, plenty of phone calls, and your best efforts to keep everyone happy.

The key to successfully coordinating any type of event, large or small, lies in the details. In a major sports event, the details can be endless: travel, lodging, and hospitality needs for the out-of-town players and staff; special banquets and breakfasts; press conferences and other activities that round out a perfect sports event. Someone has to make sure that there's plenty of parking, adequate security, and a cleanup crew in place after the game. Event planners use tools such as time lines, schedules, and checklists to keep themselves organized. Computer technology has made it much easier to manage all the details.

One of the most important parts of an event coordinator's work is solving problems before they can happen. Event coordinators do this by thinking through all the worst-case scenarios that could possibly occur, if possible, making a plan to avoid the problem altogether and, if necessary, figuring out what to do in case it does happen. This type of problem-solving action is called troubleshooting.

Most event coordinators would probably compare their jobs to being ringmasters in a three-ring circus. There's activity going on all around them, and their job is to stay focused and in control of all that's happening.

Sports event coordinators may work for a specific team, a sports facility, a government agency, or they may work for a company that specializes in event planning. As you might expect, each type of sporting event has its own unique peculiarities to contend with. For instance, someone who is organizing a major marathon has to accommodate the safety of thousands of participants over several miles of designated course. And someone who is organizing a soccer tournament has to coordinate the schedules of several teams on several fields. And don't forget the trophies!

There isn't necessarily a direct route for becoming a sports event coordinator. Some find that a college degree in an area such as sports administration, business administration, public relations, or marketing proves useful. Others find that they can get a start with an entry-level position, learn the ropes, prove their abilities, and move up to positions of greater responsibility. Volunteering is probably the one experience common to most event coordinators. Getting involved in local sports events and tournaments can provide the on-the-job training that is essential to managing a major event.

There's one more thing to keep in mind as you consider this type of career: Sports isn't the only place to put event planning skills to good use. Event planners also specialize in conventions, trade shows, business meetings, weddings, fundraisers, reunions, and parties. If lots of variety and having a good time are high on your list of job priorities, this is a career to consider.

TRY IT OUT

PARTY TIME!

The next time the Super Bowl or World Series rolls around, talk to your parents about hosting a big bash. To throw a successful party, you'll need to plan the guest list, invite the guests, plan the menu, prepare the food, and so on. Make sure you think about the details such as where everyone will sit, what to do in case of spills, and how much food you'll need. Keep track of all your plans on a master checklist. Take care of the details and on game day you can just relax and have a great time. (Remember that part of a special events coordinator's job is to make sure that all laws and regulations are honored. Keep your sports event in line.)

WORLD'S LONGEST TO-DO LIST

Imagine that you've been chosen to coordinate the All-Star football game this year. It will be held in Honolulu, Hawaii, and you are responsible for making sure that everything goes smoothly. The first thing you need to do is sit down and make a list of everything that needs to happen to assure a successful game. Don't stop until you've thought of at least 25 items that will need your attention.

WORLDWIDE CONNECTIONS

Acquaint yourself with a world-class selection of Internet resources for meeting and event planners. Visit sites such as

- ⚙ Meeting Planner (http://www.mmaweb.com/meetings), where you'll find countless links to everything from software and supplies to conference centers and travel guides
- ⚙ Event Seeker (http://www/eventseeker.com), an award-winning calendar of business and leisure events
- ⚙ Event Web (http://www/eventweb.com), an on-line newsletter offering tips and advice for event planners

CHECK IT OUT

Council of Communication Societies
P.O. Box 1074
Silver Spring, Maryland 20910

International Society of Meeting Planners
8383 East Evans Road
Scottsdale, Arizona 85260

Meeting Planners International
1950 Stemmons Freeway, Suite 5018
Dallas, Texas 75207

National Association of Athletic Marketing and Development
  Directors
Athletic Department
University of Michigan
1000 South State Street
Ann Arbor, Michigan 48109

Public Relations Society of America
33 Irving Place
New York, New York 10003

GET ACQUAINTED

Dick Ratliff, Sports Event
Coordinator

CAREER PATH

CHILDHOOD ASPIRATION: To go to college; at various times entertained thoughts of becoming a coach, a cartoonist, an architect, a teacher, and a salesman.

FIRST JOB: Making Christmas wreaths, loading them in his wagon, and selling them to neighbors when he was just a young boy.

CURRENT JOB: President of the Tournament of Roses Association.

THINGS WERE DIFFERENT THEN

Dick Ratliff graduated from high school in 1955 and says things were very different back then. For one thing, he says that there wasn't much time to think about what you wanted to do in life. It was pretty clear cut: to get a good education, to get a good job, and to raise a family. That's exactly what Ratliff did. He worked his way as a carpenter and coach through four years at the University of California at Los Angeles. He got married as a junior in college and kept on studying and working. After he earned a degree in political science, Ratliff continued working as a union carpenter for a couple of years until presented with what turned out to be the opportunity of a lifetime. That opportunity was to buy a wholesale roofing materials business. Overall, business was good through the years that he raised his family. So good that it's given him the chance to semiretire and indulge his real passion—the Tournament of Roses parade and football game.

A LABOR OF LOVE

Ratliff has been a volunteer for the Tournament of Roses parade and Rose Bowl game for more than 30 years, when he started out manning barricades at the parade. Over the years, he has served on many different committees, including the Public Relations Committee; the Coronation, Queen, and Court Committee; and the Float Committee. In several instances, he's taken on the leadership position on the committee by serving as committee chair. Now he's the president of the entire operation. Or seeing close to a thousand volunteers (donating a total of 80,000 volunteer hours each year) and handling a multimillion-dollar budget, Ratliff says his job is quite a bit like running a large corporation. The notable difference is that he doesn't receive a paycheck.

Even though Ratliff devotes between 20 to 30 hours every week to the tournament, he doesn't receive a penny in return. Ratliff says that this volunteer work has introduced him to a whole other side of life, and he's been enriched in ways that money can't buy.

As president, Ratliff is responsible for things like planning the budget, making long-range plans, and keeping in touch with the various committees that run specific aspects of the event. He spends quite a bit of time on the phone and often travels as a goodwill ambassador for the tournament. Socializing with parade corporate sponsors and big-name sports figures is just part of the job.

A FAMILY TRADITION

Ratliff learned the value of volunteering through the example of his very involved parents. His father was active as scoutmaster of his son's Boy Scout troop, in his son's high school and college sports activities, and in professional associations for his industry. His mother volunteered in cub scouts, the PTA, and business leadership. The Ratliff family tradition of volunteering has entered a third generation: One of Ratliff's sons serves as a Tournament of Roses volunteer, and the other coaches YMCA and Little League teams.

A WINNING FORMULA

Ratliff says that he still hasn't found a better way for preparing for life's challenges than by getting a good education. He credits his own liberal arts education with teaching him how to write and reason—two skills that he's put to the test in his business and in his volunteer activities.

Sports Information Director

SKILL SET

✔ SPORTS

✔ TALKING

✔ WRITING

GO to a college-level sports event and collect all the available promotional materials.

READ the sports information contained in the "virtual resource center for sports information" at http://www.sirc.ca/. With links to more than 14,000 sites, it may take a while!

TRY finding the website for a favorite college on the Internet and look for information about their sports program.

WHAT IS A SPORTS INFORMATION DIRECTOR?

Sports information directors are public relations experts who specialize in sports. Sports information directors typically represent either an entire sports program or a particular sport or team. Places that employ sports information directors include colleges and universities, professional sports teams, sports clubs and resorts, and sports associations.

The basic goal of sports information directors is to attract attention, particularly the media's attention, to their sports program. To accomplish this, sports information directors write and distribute a variety of newsworthy materials, including team and player biographies, press kits, yearbooks, game programs, and press releases.

Newsworthy events may take the form of game announcements, team statistics, introductions of new players or coaching staff, and other types of factual information. Sports information directors may also try to "get some ink" with interesting feature stories about individual players or teams or by suggesting angles for stories about team trivia, traditions, or other unusual ideas.

Another area of responsibility that generally falls under a sports information director's care is arranging press conferences, press briefings, and interviews. These kinds of face-to-face informational events occur before and/or after games and when other matters of interest to the public arise (such as a player trade or a coach firing). Usually the sports information director also is responsible for coordinating details associated with televising or providing live radio broadcasts of games.

As with any other public relations person, a sports information director must be prepared to handle crisis situations. For instance, if a player gets injured or in some sort of trouble, a sports information director must be ready to provide reliable and objective information. Sometimes things happen so fast that he or she must be ready to respond to a situation immediately, making effective verbal communication skills very important.

Along with all their work building and maintaining good relations with the media, sports information directors must also satisfy another group: sports fans. Sports information directors produce game programs and other materials that keep fans informed and excited about the team. They may also work with the marketing department to prepare promotional materials announcing games and other sports events.

This job involves a lot of responsibility, and it can be quite demanding. This career works best for someone who loves sports and enjoys being in the thick of things. Preparing to be a sports information director should include college-level training in a field such as public relations, communications, journalism, or marketing.

TRY IT OUT

SPREAD THE WORD

Here are number of ways to serve as your school's sports information director:

- make posters promoting an upcoming sports event
- write a story about a star player and submit it to the local newspaper
- put together a special game program for the homecoming game
- interview the coach for an article in the school newspaper
- create a collage celebrating your school's sports programs (use photographs, headlines, scores from big wins, etc.)

JUST THE FACTS, PLEASE

Pick a favorite professional athlete. Collect as much information as you can about him or her, including photographs from magazine or newspaper articles. Use this information to write a player biography. Make sure to include important details such as age, hometown, college attended, and key achievements as an athlete. Use a computer to jazz it up and make it look professional.

THE YEAR IN REVIEW

Volunteer to work as (or with) the sports editor for the school yearbook. That experience will help you get a look at all the sports programs at your school and to find creative ways of presenting them in print.

CHECK IT OUT

College Sports Information Directors of America
Campus Box 114
Texas A&M University
Kingsville, Texas 78363

International Public Relations Association
250 West Floresta Way
Menlo Park, California 94005

National Association of Athletic Marketing and
  Development Directors
Athletic Department
University of Michigan
1000 South State Street
Ann Arbor, Michigan 48109

Public Relations Society of America
33 Irving Place
New York, New York 10003

GET ACQUAINTED

Bob Beretta, Sports
Information Director

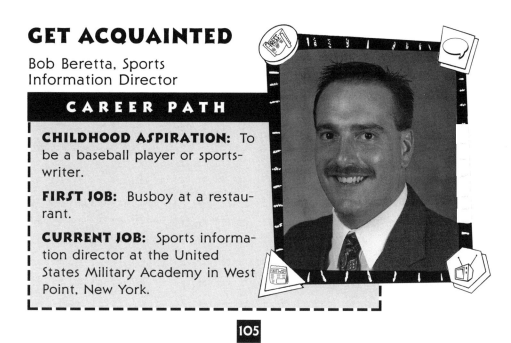

CAREER PATH

CHILDHOOD ASPIRATION: To be a baseball player or sportswriter.

FIRST JOB: Busboy at a restaurant.

CURRENT JOB: Sports information director at the United States Military Academy in West Point, New York.

A HEAD START

Bob Beretta got an early start on his career. When he was just eight or nine years old, he would come home from his Little League games and write extensive notes about how the game went. He still has notebooks full of these stories as well as his personal accounts of World Series games and other major league action. Of course, at the time, he had no idea that this was something he could do for a living. It was just something he did for fun.

GOOD-BYE BASEBALL, HELLO SPORTS INFORMATION

When it came time to go to college, Beretta went with high hopes of becoming a professional baseball player. As backup, he pursued a degree in mass communications that gave him a chance to work on Plan B—becoming a sportswriter. Unfortunately, an elbow injury that required surgery dashed his hopes of going pro; however, he had inadvertently discovered a new "ballgame" in the school's sports information office. The part of the job that really clicked with him was that instead of reporting about teams as an outsider, he was actually promoting them as an insider. It allowed him to stay closer to the game and really get to know the athletes.

He'd been working on the school newspaper all along with the assumption that he'd look for a job as a sportswriter for a newspaper or magazine. When a friend of his talked him into helping out in the sports information office, Beretta discovered the perfect way to blend his love of sports and writing. He spent his spare time learning all he could about the job and completed a summer internship at the military academy in West Point.

TIMING IS EVERYTHING

West Point is one of the first places he looked for a job after graduating. It was located close to where he grew up (Beretta has fond memories of attending army football and baseball games with his father), and he'd already had a chance to prove himself during his internship. Fortunately, the time was right for them to expand their office, so they hired him as an assistant. When his boss left for another position, Beretta was promoted to sports information director, and he's been there ever since.

WHO'S COUNTING?

Beretta's office acts as the official publicists for all of West Point's 25 intercollegiate sports. That means Beretta himself and his four assistants cover everything from football, baseball, and basketball to rifle, volleyball, lacrosse, and gymnastics. Some sports have a men's and women's team. The National Collegiate Athletic Association (NCAA) rules for several sports such as football and baseball mandate that someone from Beretta's staff actually attend the games wherever they are—in town or across the country.

For other sports, the staff is able to get final scores and a game summary from the coaches. Regardless of how they get the information, the sports information office prepares a media release for each and every game. In 1997, they estimated that they sent out a total of 482 game stories. That's not to mention the multipage game notes that they prepare and release prior to many of the games and the 200-page (or so) football media guide that they prepare each fall.

Beretta says that his job boils down to one thing: good writing. Anyone who wants to follow in his footsteps needs to know how to write—accurately, with great attention to detail, and quickly.

YES, SIR!

The United States Military Academy is a prestigious college that trains young men and women to become army officers. That makes Beretta's job a little different from the typical college. He has learned to be sensitive to military protocol and to honor the military's chain of command. For a firsthand look at West Point's sports program, check out Beretta's office's webpage at http://www.usma.edu/athletics.

Sports Pro

WHAT IS A SPORTS PRO?

A successful sports professional, or pro, has to be good enough at his or her chosen sport to wow seasoned athletes and patient enough to teach first-time players. Those are the key requirements for becoming a sports pro. Sports pros work at resorts or clubs and teach a particular sport such as golf, tennis, swimming, or skiing.

Sports pros can work with individuals or groups, children or adults. They must be able to instruct, evaluate, and advise both beginners and experts on how to improve their game or skills. A training session with a sports pro generally consists of three parts: a demonstration of the required skills, an explanation of the rules, and an overview of basic safety precautions. After that it's practice, practice, and more practice on specific skills.

The ability to get along with others and communicate effectively are skills that are just as important as athletic ability in this people-oriented business. Sports pros have to keep their students motivated to work hard and challenged to push themselves to improve.

Training other trainers is often part of the job for the more experienced sports pro. Other advanced opportunities for sports pros include running the administrative side of a training program or supervising other instructors.

Certain types of sports such as diving, hiking, and cycling lend themselves to other types of ventures for sports pros (and fanatics). Such ventures include organizing tours and special trips for both beginners and more advanced learners.

A sports pro can also be a personal trainer who designs personalized fitness programs for individual people. Taking into consideration a person's fitness level, eating habits, and overall lifestyle, trainers create an individual workout plan and keep their clients motivated to stick with it.

Some of the very best trainers work with some of the very best athletes to train for competitions such as the Olympics. They work one-on-one with individual athletes and implement ongoing and intense training regimens. Working at this level of competition requires full-time commitment, as the trainer is often responsible for the athlete's overall physical conditioning and training, motivation, and even nutrition programs.

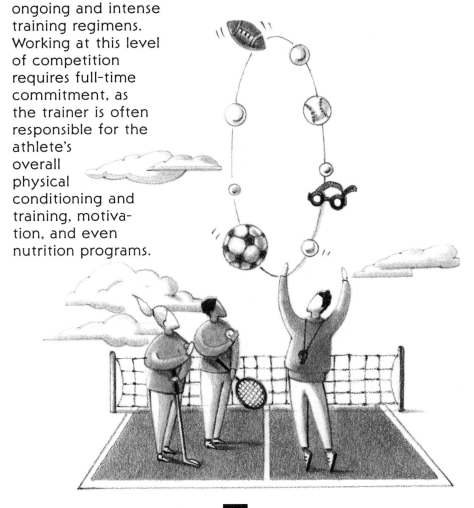

TRY IT OUT

JOIN THE CLUB

The best advice for would-be sports pros is to dedicate your-self to a sport you enjoy most and play best. If your game is golf, play golf. If your sport is tennis, play tennis. If it's skiing, ski. If your school has a team or club for any of these sports—join it. Learn all you can.

Remember, you have to be *very* good at your sport to be a sports pro. Enter tournaments and contests. Play on your school team. The more you play, the better you get. The better you get, the easier it will be to teach others to play.

CLIMB THE LADDER OF SUCCESS

There aren't many junior high or senior high kids who can walk into a resort or country club and get a job as a sports pro. But they can walk in and get a job as a caddy, gift shop clerk, or dishwasher. Getting entry-level jobs in places that also employ sports pros lets you start learning while you're earning. Watch how they work with people, observe their own practice sessions, and ask as many questions as you can.

BE A WALKING SPORTS ENCYCLOPEDIA

Part of a sports pro's job is to keep students entertained. Since the pro and the student share a common interest in the sport, it's important to keep up with what's happening and who's doing what so that there's always plenty to talk about.

There are several ways to build your storehouse of knowl-edge. Read the newspapers and sports magazines (*Sports Illustrated* is one of the best in comprehensive coverage of major sports). Watch sports broadcasts on the news and fre-quent cable channels such as ESPN.

Or, if you have access to a computer, tap into the Internet and visit these sites for up-to-the-minute sports news:

 ☼ http://www.espn.com
 ☼ http://www.sportsillustrated.com

CHECK IT OUT

American Alliance for Health, Physical Education, Recreation
and Dance
1900 Association Drive
Reston, Virginia 22091

Athletic Institute
200 Castlewood Drive
North Palm Beach, Florida 33408

International Association of Fitness Professionals
6190 Cornerstone Court East, Suite 204
San Diego, California 92121-3773

Professional Ski Instructors of America
1323 South Van Gordon, Suite 101
Lakewood, Colorado 80228

GET ACQUAINTED

Andy Johnson, Sports
Professional

CAREER PATH

CHILDHOOD ASPIRATION: To
be a state patrolman.

FIRST JOB: Worked for the
Seattle ski patrol.

CURRENT JOB: Technical director for a Washington ski school.

KID ON SKIS

Andy Johnson started skiing when he was eight years old.
Since skiing is an expensive sport, he got a job with the ski
patrol when he was 16 so that he could get a free ski pass

every weekend. He later became one of the youngest ski instructors working for the Shoreline (Washington) school district. Once he graduated from high school, he headed to Colorado for what was supposed to be a two-year stint as a professional ski instructor.

The idea was to get skiing out of his system and then go back home and attend school to become a state patrolman. That was several years ago. Although Johnson has since returned to the Seattle area, he's still on the slopes and showing no signs of slowing down.

Coming home has provided Johnson opportunities to advance his skiing career to the point that his main responsibility is training other trainers. He says that since the Seattle ski industry is so much smaller than Colorado's, it is less competitive and has given him the chance to take on a leadership position.

Most of Johnson's skiing experience has come from being on the slopes year in and year out. He's taken several training clinics to learn how to teach and has discovered that he has a knack for working with people.

ONE SKIER'S IDEA OF PARADISE

Johnson's idea of paradise would be year-round skiing. You'd think that since skiing is a winter sport requiring lots of snow such an idea would be little more than wishful thinking. However, Johnson has found a way to beat Mother Nature at her own game. For a couple of years, he taught skiing in Colorado during the November to April snow season and then headed off to New Zealand to teach skiing during the May to September winter months. It was perfect, he says.

DON'T GIVE UP YOUR DAY JOB

Ski instructors have a job only when there is snow on the ground. Unless you chase winter around the globe like Johnson has in the past, most ski instructors need skills to earn a living in the off-season.

Johnson's theory is that hard work and an entrepreneurial spirit are the keys to success when he's not skiing. He's putting all his people skills to good work by pursuing an off-season career in sales and marketing.

ADVICE TO FUTURE SPORTS PROS

Deciding to become a sports professional is more than a career choice; it's a lifestyle choice. For instance, skiers really have to enjoy working outside in winter weather and living in a small town or resort area. Fortunately, Johnson thrives on it all—the cold nose, the mountains, and the look of snow-laden trees. He can't imagine not doing what he does.

Johnson says that you've got to know your sport and love it. But even more important, you've got to know how to deal with people and enjoy working with them. Ski schools can train you to be a better skier. You have to learn how to treat students well all on your own.

TAKE A TRIP!

Sportswriter

✔ SPORTS
✔ TRAVELING
✔ WRITING

GO join the school newspaper or yearbook club.

READ some of the well-written sports articles in *USA Today* and *Sports Illustrated*.

TRY getting involved in sports—playing them, watching them, and reading about them.

WHAT IS A SPORTSWRITER?

Sportswriters are journalists who attend sports events and write stories about what happens. They interview players and coaches, keep track of wins and losses, and research background information. Sportswriters may report on stories for print media, such as small or large newspapers, magazines, or on-line news services. Other sports journalists report on sports events for broadcast media such as television or radio.

As other types of reporters do, sportswriters generally work on two types of stories. Beat writers cover certain teams or certain sports and report day-of-the-game stories. They have to stay on top of breaking news and write pieces that are interesting, informative, and accurate. Larger papers or television stations assign specific "beats" for specific journalists to cover. Obviously, the more experience and talent a reporter has, the more exciting assignments he or she receives.

Columnists write feature stories and opinion pieces about their area of expertise. Instead of covering specific games, they might write about specific players or the sports industry in general. Creativity and a nose for news are key skills of a good columnist.

While deadlines come quickly for all types of sports journalists, there is even more pressure on broadcast reporters who often must provide on-the-spot coverage and analysis of various sporting events. With little time to organize their thoughts and no time to edit out mistakes, these reporters must think fast on their feet and have an in-depth knowledge of the sport and the players that they are reporting about.

Similar to other types of journalists, those who specialize in sports generally have a college degree in an area such as journalism, mass communication, or English. Getting as much on-the-job experience as possible while getting an education helps always to boost the résumé.

Sportswriting is a fast-paced and competitive game. It's just the job for inquisitive sports fans who can sniff out a story and write it so well that readers find it the next best thing to being there themselves.

TRY IT OUT

PLAY BALL

Tennis, basketball, baseball, soccer, football—play as many sports as you can as often as possible learn the ropes about sports and teamwork.

THE WRITE STUFF

Two ideas here. First, pick up a sports beat for an already established school or community newspaper. You may have to start by submitting stories on events that aren't covered by the regular newspapers. Prove that you are dependable, and learn how to write interesting stories about sports events. If you are persistent, you may land yourself your first published byline.

The second idea is for the more adventurous at heart. Check out the various sports leagues in your community. How does one team find out how well another is doing? Who keeps track of games and tournaments? Is there any place where a parent might find news about budding sports pros? Find out if any of these groups might be interested in a regular newsletter about their teams and games. If so, cover as many games as you can, cultivate contacts with each team to find out scores and highlights of games you miss, and write some interesting stories about players and coaches.

Use your computer to produce a great-looking publications, and you'll get some great experience as a sports journalist. Play your cards right, and you might also find a way to make this little venture profitable by selling subscriptions.

TALK THE TALK

Have you ever noticed how many unusual ways sportscasters have of saying the same thing? A team doesn't win a game; they "dominate" it. The other team doesn't lose the game; they're "creamed" or "decimated."

Get a notebook and keep a log of the phrases you hear on the news and read in the paper. Keep your collection handy, and use them to spice up your own reports.

ROUND-THE-CLOCK COVERAGE

Log on the Internet anytime, day or night, for the latest sports news. Here are some sites to visit first for a look at the world of sports:

- ☼ http://www.sportsillustrated.com
- ☼ http://www.espn.com

The following websites will take you to directly to the national headquarters of some of your favorite sports leagues:

- ☼ http://www.afl.com
- ☼ http://www.nba.com
- ☼ http://www.nfl.com
- ☼ http://www.nhl.com

CHECK IT OUT

American Sportscasters Association
150 Nassau Street
New York, New York 10038

Dow Jones Newspaper Fund
P.O. Box 300
Princeton, New Jersey 08543
(To order a copy of *The Journalist's Road to Success: A Career and Scholarship Guide*, call 800-DOWFUND.)

National Newspaper Association
1627 K Street NW
Washington, D.C. 20006

Newspaper Association of America
11600 Sunrise Valley Drive
Reston, Virginia 22091

Newspaper Guild
R&I Department
8611 Second Street NW
Silver Spring, Maryland 20910

Society for Professional Journalism
P.O. Box 77
Greencastle, Indiana 46135

GET ACQUAINTED

Debbie Becker, Journalist

CAREER PATH

CHILDHOOD ASPIRATION: To be a forest ranger.

FIRST JOB: Worked as a gofer for the *Washington Post.*

CURRENT JOB: Sports reporter for *USA Today.*

Debbie Becker and friend at the 1998 Winter Olympics in Japan.

THE RIGHT PLACE AT THE RIGHT TIME

Along with a talent for writing and knowledge of a number of sports, Debbie Becker also has a knack for being in the right place at the right time. She landed a job with the *Washington Post* by joking with a friend to put in a good word for her with his editor. He did, and she got a job.

USA Today was just a new, upstart newspaper when Becker graduated from college. Today the paper is read by some 2 million readers every weekday.

ME AND MY BIG MOUTH!

As a freshman hockey player at the American University in Washington, D.C., Becker was disappointed to find out that the school paper covered only men's sports events. When she went to the office to complain, she found out that the only reason women's sports weren't covered was because there was no one to write the stories. Becker volunteered to start reporting about these neglected events, discovered she liked it, and a career was born.

Sports is still a male-dominated world, and Becker often finds herself the only woman in the press box at many events. To get where she is today, Becker has had to work extra hard and watch her step, but she wouldn't trade the experience for anything.

OLYMPIC-SIZED BEAT

Becker has reported on the Winter Olympics in Calgary, the Summer Olympics in Barcelona, and the Summer Olympics in Atlanta. She specializes in covering gymnastics, figure skating, and cycling events. This beat involves more than just covering the Olympic games. Long before the world gathers to compete, there are trials and national championships to keep track of. Becker particularly likes doing stories on unknown athletes in minor sports and on women athletes because it gives her a chance to recognize people who've worked hard and are often overlooked.

THIS JOB HAS PERKS

Olympics, World Series, Super Bowl—Becker has been there, done that, seen it. As a journalist, Becker gets to see for free events that other people have to pay lots of money for, if they can tickets at all.

ADVICE TO FUTURE SPORTS JOURNALISTS

Get all the internship experience you can so that you can find out what you like and what you're good at. Becker had originally planned to get into television broadcasting, but an internship experience taught her that she didn't like it at all, so she refocused her attention on newspapers.

Trainer

WHAT IS A TRAINER?

Wherever there are people playing sports, there are people getting hurt. A look at annual statistics indicates that millions of people get hurt every year playing everything from bowling to soccer to wrestling. In many cases, especially in organized sports programs, an athletic trainer is the first person on the scene to evaluate and begin treating sports-related injuries. Cool, calm, and collected are words that describe the best trainers in these types of crisis situations.

Along with providing on-the-scene assistance to injured players, trainers are also involved in important ways before and after injuries occur. The top priority of every athletic trainer is to prevent injuries from ever happening. They do this by making sure that the athletes are in peak physical condition, that they are getting the strengthening and conditioning exercises they need, and that their diets support the special demands their profession puts on their bodies.

Trainers also have important responsibilities after someone is injured. For one thing, a trainer may act as a liaison between the athlete and the medical professionals who treat the injuries. It is often up to the trainer to help an athlete understand the nature of the injury and offer guidance in making important decisions about the best medical options. Sometimes, it means being on hand to provide support and encouragement during painful surgeries and other treatments. After the medical professionals do all they can, a trainer steps in to help get the athlete back in the game. This process may involve special physical therapy sessions, heat, whirlpool, or massage treatments.

While it is ultimately up to the player to decide when to return to the game, most players count on unbiased recommendations from the team doctor and trainer about when the time is right. Ultimately, it is up to the trainer to decide when and if a player is ready to play. One of the biggest ethical dilemmas a trainer may face is keeping players off the roster until their bodies are completely healed in spite of intense pressure to get them back in action. With some players being crucial to the game, some trainers might be tempted to rush the rehabilitation process.

Athletic trainers are employed in high schools, colleges, universities, and professional sports teams. Most trainers at the high school level also teach or coach at least part-time.

Other trainers work in sports centers or clinics helping treat the 18 million or so people that are injured each year playing sports. With more than $10 billion being spent on rehabilitation programs alone (not including surgery, treatment, and prevention), there is plenty of opportunity for well-trained and committed sports medicine professionals.

To become an officially recognized athletic trainer, you must be certified by the National Athletic Trainers Association. This requires earning a college degree in a field such as physical education, kinesiology (the study of body movement and anatomy), coaching, or sports medicine as well as meeting some very specific internship requirements and passing some special tests. It helps if you start college with a pretty good idea that you want to become an athletic trainer so that you can complete the internship requirement while you earn your degree.

While athletic trainers might seem the most obvious job in sports medicine, there are other options you might want to consider, including physical therapist, nutritionist, or kinesiologist. In addition, many full-fledged medical doctors and dentists devote themselves to the practice of sports-related medicine.

TRY IT OUT

THE SPORTS DOCTOR IS IN

Thanks to the ingenuity of a company called MedFacts, you don't have to wait any longer to start working as a sports medicine professional. Their interactive website, Sports Doc, gives you the chance to diagnose and treat an amusing assortment of patients with sports-related injuries. You can play sports doctor at http://www.medfacts.com/sprtsdoc. htm.

WEB RESOURCES FOR TRAINERS

The Internet provides easy access to sports medicine information, athletic trainers, and actual training programs. Start your Internet investigation with visits to sites such as:

☀ The National Athletic Trainers Association home page at http://www.nata.org is a good source of career information and other special features.

☀ Medicine in Sports Pages on the Web at http://www.mspweb.com provides links to all kinds of websites, including magazines and journals, schools and universities, and clinics and practices.

☀ Be among the first to know about new injury prevention and treatment techniques at http:/www.ivanhoe.com/sportsmed where breakthrough medical news from the world's leading medical centers and research labs is shared.

GET A HEAD START ON THE ACTION

Do you have what it takes to be an athletic trainer? Find out now by getting involved in your school or community recreation sports programs. Talk to the coach or athletic director to see where he or she needs the most help.

Before you get started, you'll have to learn some basics. You can do this by taking a first aid and perhaps even a CPR course through the American Red Cross. Look in the white pages for the phone number of the local office.

CHECK IT OUT

Amateur Athletic Trainers Association
660 West Duarte Road
Arcadia, California 91006

American Medical Athletic Association
P.O. Box 4704
North Hollywood, California 91423

International Center for Sports Nutrition
502 South 44th Street
Omaha, Nebraska 68105

National Athletic Health Association
660 West Duarte Road
Arcadia, California 91006

National Athletic Trainers Association
2952 Stemmons, Suite 200
Dallas, Texas 75247

National Athletic Trainers Association Board of Certification
3725 National Drive, Suite 213
Raleigh, North Carolina 27612

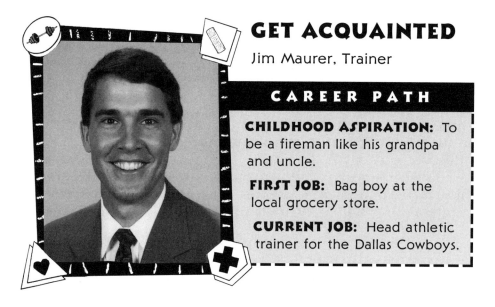

GET ACQUAINTED

Jim Maurer, Trainer

CAREER PATH

CHILDHOOD ASPIRATION: To be a fireman like his grandpa and uncle.

FIRST JOB: Bag boy at the local grocery store.

CURRENT JOB: Head athletic trainer for the Dallas Cowboys.

A BIG BROTHER'S ADVICE

Jim Maurer says that he wouldn't be where he is today if it weren't for some advice his big brother, Bob, gave him when he was a sophomore in high school. The advice? Get off your duff and do something! It seems that Maurer had spent freshman year in high school just going to school, getting pretty good grades, and hanging out. His older and wiser brother knew that he was missing out on some of the best parts of high school, so he hooked Maurer up with the school's athletic director and got him involved with the sports program.

As it turns out, Maurer was good at math, so the athletic director put him to work keeping team statistics at football games. Later, he was asked to be the assistant trainer so that someone would be ready to take over for the senior who was the team manager. His school sent him to a Cramer workshop at Southern Methodist University (SMU) where he spent two weeks learning the basics: first aid, taping ankles, etc. This training prepared him to finish out high school as the football team manager.

IT'S NOT ALWAYS THIS EASY

When it came time to decide where to go to college, he choose SMU with hopes of becoming an athletic trainer. It helped that his stepsister, a nurse, was already a trainer there. He is grateful to have had the chance to learn under one of the best in the business, Cash Birdwell, who has been at SMU for more than 30 years.

He started the required trainer internship as an assistant trainer for both the football and swim teams. During his junior year, he got the lucky break that set the course for his professional career. He was chosen for a student internship with the Dallas Cowboys at their training camp. His senior year, he had the chance to intern with the Kansas City Chiefs. As if that weren't enough, after he'd graduated from college and was busy earning his teaching credentials, he was chosen to participate in the Cowboys' graduate assistant program for two years in a row. By this time, Maurer's foot was planted firmly in the door, and it was an easy decision for the Cowboys to name him an official assistant trainer when the position became available.

Needless to say, Maurer has been with the Cowboys ever since. He says he was one of the lucky ones. Most people don't land a job with the pros right out of college. In fact, his all-time goal as an aspiring athletic trainer in college had been to land a spot with one of the top *college* teams.

ALL IN A DAY'S WORK

Maurer does his best to keep the Cowboys healthy and injury-free. When the inevitable injuries come, his job is to get those million-dollar men back into tip-top shape and out on the playing field as quickly and as safely as possible. He's standing by at all the games and practices to provide emergency medical attention, and quite often he's nearby when one of the players has to have surgery. Since there are usually at least 6 to 12 players in need of surgical repair after each season, his presence at their operations can become a big part of the off-season job. He serves as a liaison between the player and medical professionals, explains the ramifications of the injury to each player, and helps plan a rehabilitation program that gets players back in the game with all body parts in good working order.

HOME FOR THE HOLIDAYS

The job requires long hours and a demanding schedule. He says that he recently spent Christmas with his family for the first time in seven years. During football season, his work schedule is at least 12 hours a day, 7 days a week. He goes on the road with the team for games and attends the six-week training camp. You've got to love the work to keep up the pace.

THE HEALING TOUCH

Maurer says that what makes his work so worthwhile is being part of the success stories. Two of his favorites involve Michael Irvin and Erik Williams. He counts it a real thrill to have seen Irvin come back to be voted MVP at a Pro Bowl after recovering from a career-threatening knee injury. As for Williams, not only was it a miracle that he even survived the car crash that shattered his leg, but he also came back to play in a Pro Bowl. Success stories like this are what his job is all about.

ON THE INJURED LIST

Maurer says that it can be tough for a big, strong athlete to get used to the idea of being hurt. He jokes that the bigger they are, the harder they fall. Part of his job is to encourage injured players and motivate them to work hard throughout the often painful rehabilitation process. He's made it a point to extend the same level of care and concern to every player who gets hurt, whether it's Troy Aikman or a third-string running back.

SOME WINNING WORDS

No matter what career path a person chooses, Maurer says that the ultimate goal should be to wake up each morning and want to go to work. When work becomes something a person dreads, Maurer says it's time to find another job. Sounds like winning advice from a man who's gone with the Cowboys to the Super Bowl three times!

MAKE A SPORTY DETOUR!

Becoming a professional sports player is just one way to build a career around sports. You can add a sports element to virtually any job you might choose. For instance, accountants can work for sports teams, doctors can specialize in sports medicine, retailers can sell sports equipment and uniforms, and so on. In addition, there are quite a number of careers where a particular sport or team is central to the job. Play around with some of the following sports career ideas.

A WORLD OF SPORTS CAREERS

JOIN THE TEAM

Here are a few jobs where a particular sport (or a number of sports) is the name of the game. Each offers a unique way to make sports a central focus of your career without actually playing the game yourself.

athletic director
cheerleader
coach
equipment manager
official
referee

scoreboard operator
scout
sports administrator
team manager
umpire

MAKE SPORTS YOUR BUSINESS

In the area of business, again sports are front and center. The catch is that your business savvy and other professional skills have as much or more to do with your success in these careers as does your love of sports.

agent
business manager
equipment designer
event coordinator
health club manager
marketing director
retailer
sports store manager
ticket manager

SPREAD THE WORD

Pick one of these jobs and you won't have to keep quiet about being a sports fanatic. Each requires a special ability to articulate the finer points of the game.

announcer
broadcaster
journalist

photographer
sportscaster

TEACH IT

What better way to share your love of a particular sport than to teach others how to enjoy it. Here are just a few ideas to get you thinking.

aerobics instructor
aquatics specialist
dance instructor
fitness trainer
gymnastics instructor

lifeguard
nutritionist
personal trainer
physical education teacher
sports pro

ADVENTURE IN THE GREAT OUTDOORS

Just in case you are one of those sports fanatics who prefer hanging out in the great outdoors to the gym, here are a couple of ideas to consider.

camp director
ecotourism developer
fish and game warden

forester
park ranger
river guide

INFORMATION IS POWER

Mind-boggling, isn't it? There are so many great choices, so many jobs you've never heard of before. How will you ever narrow it down to the perfect spot for you?

First, pinpoint the ideas that sound the most interesting to you. Then, find out all you can about them. As you may have noticed, a similar pattern of information was used for each of the career entries included in this book. Each entry included

💡 a general description or definition of the career

💡 some hands-on projects that give readers a chance to actually experience a job

💡 a list of organizations to contact for more information

💡 an interview with a professional

You can use information like this to help you determine the best career path to pursue. Since there isn't room in one book to profile all these sports-related career choices, here's your chance to do it yourself. Conduct a full investigation into a sports career that interests you.

Please Note: If this book does not belong to you use a separate sheet of paper to record your responses to the following questions.

CAREER TITLE_____

WHAT IS A _____?
Use career encyclopedias and other resources to write a description of this career.

_____
_____
_____

TRY IT OUT
Write project ideas here. Ask your parents and your teacher to come up with a plan.

_____
_____
_____

CHECK IT OUT
List professional organizations where you can learn more about this profession.

_____
_____
_____

GET ACQUAINTED
Interview a professional in the field and summarize your findings.

_____
_____
_____

DON'T STOP NOW!
GO FOR IT!

It's been a fast-paced trip so far. Take a break, regroup, and look at all the progress you've made.

1st Stop: Self-Discovery
You discovered some personal interests and natural abilities that you can start building a career around.

2nd Stop: Exploration
You've explored an exciting array of career opportunities in sports. You're now aware that your career can involve either a specialized area with many educational requirements or that it can involve a practical application of skills with a minimum of training and experience.

At this point, you've found a couple of (or few) careers that really intrigue you. Now it's time to put it all together and do all you can to make an informed, intelligent choice. It's time to move on.

DON'T STOP NOW! GO FOR IT!

3rd Stop: Experimentation

By the time you finish this section, you'll have reached one of three points in the career planning process.

1. **Green light!** You found it. No need to look any further. This is *the* career for you. (This may happen to a lucky few. Don't worry if it hasn't happened yet for you. This whole process is about exploring options, experimenting with ideas, and, eventually, making the best choice for you.)

2. **Yellow light!** Close, but not quite. You seem to be on the right path but you haven't nailed things down for sure. (This is where many people your age end up, and it's a good place to be. You've learned what it takes to really check things out. Hang in there. Your time will come.)

3. **Red light!** Whoa! No doubt about it, this career just isn't for you. (Congratulations! Aren't you glad you found out now and not after you'd spent four years in college preparing for this career? Your next stop: Make a U-turn and start this process over with another career.)

Here's a sneak peek at what you'll be doing in the next section.

☼ First, you'll pick a favorite career idea (or two or three).

☼ Second, you'll snoop around the library to find answers to the 10 things you've just got to know about your future career.

☼ Third, you'll pick up the phone and talk to someone whose career you admire to find out what it's really like.

☼ Fourth, you'll link up with a whole world of great information about your career idea on the Internet (it's easier than you think).

☼ Fifth, you'll go on the job to shadow a professional for a day.

Hang on to your hats and get ready to make tracks!

#1 NARROW DOWN YOUR CHOICES

You've been introduced to quite a few sports career ideas. You may also have some ideas of your own to add. Which ones appeal to you the most?

Write your top three choices in the spaces below. (Sorry if this is starting to sound like a broken record, but . . . if this book does not belong to you, write your responses on a separate sheet of paper.)

1. _____

2. _____

3. _____

#2 SNOOP AT THE LIBRARY

Take your list of favorite career ideas, a notebook, and a helpful adult with you to the library. When you get there, go to the reference section and ask the librarian to help you find

books about careers. Most libraries will have at least one set of career encyclopedias. Some of the larger libraries may also have career information on CD-ROM.

Gather all the information you can and use it to answer the following questions in your notebook about each of the careers on your list. Make sure to ask for help if you get stuck.

TOP 10 THINGS YOU NEED TO KNOW ABOUT YOUR CAREER

1. What kinds of skills does this job require?
2. What kind of training is required? (Compare the options for a high school degree, trade school degree, two-year degree, four-year degree, and advanced degree.)
3. What types of classes do I need to take in high school in order to be accepted into a training program?
4. What are the names of three schools or colleges where I can get the training I need?
5. Are there any apprenticeship or internship opportunities available? If so, where? If not, could I create my own opportunity? How?
6. How much money can I expect to earn as a beginner? How much with more experience?
7. What kinds of places hire people to do this kind of work?
8. What is a typical work environment like? For example, would I work in a busy office, outdoors, or in a laboratory?
9. What are some books and magazines I could read to learn more about this career? Make a list and look for them at your library.
10. Where can I write for more information? Make a list of professional associations.

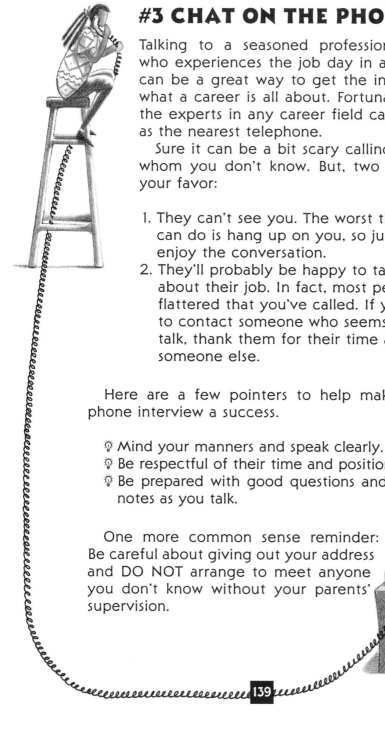

#3 CHAT ON THE PHONE

Talking to a seasoned professional—someone who experiences the job day in and day out—can be a great way to get the inside story on what a career is all about. Fortunately for you, the experts in any career field can be as close as the nearest telephone.

Sure it can be a bit scary calling up an adult whom you don't know. But, two things are in your favor:

1. They can't see you. The worst thing they can do is hang up on you, so just relax and enjoy the conversation.
2. They'll probably be happy to talk to you about their job. In fact, most people will be flattered that you've called. If you happen to contact someone who seems reluctant to talk, thank them for their time and try someone else.

Here are a few pointers to help make your telephone interview a success.

- ♀ Mind your manners and speak clearly.
- ♀ Be respectful of their time and position.
- ♀ Be prepared with good questions and take notes as you talk.

One more common sense reminder: Be careful about giving out your address and DO NOT arrange to meet anyone you don't know without your parents' supervision.

TRACKING DOWN CAREER EXPERTS

You might be wondering by now how to find someone to interview. Have no fear! It's easy, if you're persistent. All you have to do is ask. Ask the right people and you'll have a great lead in no time.

A few of the people to ask and sources to turn to are

Your parents. They may know someone (or know someone who knows someone) who has just the kind of job you're looking for.

Your friends and neighbors. You might be surprised to find out how many interesting jobs these people have when you start asking them what they (or their parents) do for a living.

Librarians. Since you've already figured out what kinds of companies employ people in your field of interest, the next step is to ask for information about local employers. Although it's a bit cumbersome to use, a big volume called *Contacts Influential* can provide this kind of information.

Professional associations. Call or write to the professional associations you discovered in Activity #1 a few pages back and ask for recommendations.

Chambers of commerce. The local chamber of commerce probably has a directory of employers, their specialties, and their phone numbers. Call the chamber, explain what you are looking for, and give them a chance to help their future workforce.

Newspaper and magazine articles. Find an article about the subject you are interested in. Chances are pretty good that it will mention the name of at least one expert in the field. The article probably won't include the person's phone number (that would be too easy), so you'll have to look for clues. Common clues include the name of the company that they work for, the town that they live in, and if the person is an author, the name of their publisher. Make a few phone calls and track them down (if long distance calls are involved, make sure to get your parents' permission first).

INQUIRING KIDS WANT TO KNOW

Before you make the call, make a list of questions to ask. You'll cover more ground if you focus on using the five w's (and the h) that you've probably heard about in your creative writing classes: Who? What? Where? When? How? and Why? For example,

1. Who do you work for?
2. What is a typical work day like for you?
3. Where can I get some on-the-job experience?
4. When did you become a _____ ?
   (profession)
5. How much can you earn in this profession? (But, remember it's not polite to ask someone how much *he* or *she* earns.)
6. Why did you choose this profession?

One last suggestion: Add a professional (and very classy) touch to the interview process by following up with a thank-you note to the person who took time out of a busy schedule to talk with you.

#4 SURF THE NET

With the Internet, the new information super-highway, charging full steam ahead, you literally have a world of information at your fingertips. The Internet has something for everyone, and it's getting easier to access all the time. An increasing number of libraries and schools are offering access to the Internet on their computers. In addition, companies such as America Online and CompuServe have made it possible for anyone with a home computer to surf the World Wide Web.

A typical career search will land everything from the latest news on developments in the field and course notes from universities to museum exhibits, interactive games, educational activities, and more. You just can't beat the timeliness or the variety of information available on the Net.

One of the easiest ways to track down this information is to use an Internet search engine, such as Yahoo! Simply type in the topic you are looking for, and in a matter of seconds, you'll have a list of options from around the world. It's fun to browse—you never know what you'll come up with.

To narrow down your search a bit, look for specific websites, forums, or chatrooms that are related to your topic in the following publications:

———

Hahn, Harley. *The Internet Yellow Pages.* Berkeley, Calif.: Osborne McGraw Hill, 1997.
———. *The World Wide Web Yellow Pages.* Berkeley, Calif.: Osborne McGraw Hill, 1997.

———

To go on-line at home you may want to compare two of the more popular on-line services: America Online and CompuServe. Please note that there is a monthly subscription fee for using these services. There can also be extra fees attached to specific forums and services, so *make sure you have your parents' OK before you sign up.* For information about America Online call 800-827-6364. For information about CompuServe call 800-848-8990. Both services frequently offer free start-up deals, so shop around.

There are also many other services, depending on where you live. Check your local phone book or ads in local computer magazines for other service options.

Before you link up, keep in mind that many of these sites are geared toward professionals who are already working in a particular field. Some of the sites can get pretty technical. Just use the experience as a chance to nose around the field, hang out with the people who are tops in the field, and think about whether or not you'd like to be involved in a profession like that.

Specific sites to look for are the following:

Professional associations. Find out about what's happening in the field, conferences, journals, and other helpful tidbits.

Schools that specialize in this area. Many include research tools, introductory courses, and all kinds of interesting information.

Government agencies. Quite a few are going high-tech with lots of helpful resources.

Websites hosted by experts in the field (this seems to be a popular hobby among many professionals). These websites are often as entertaining as they are informative.

If you're not sure where to go, just start clicking around. Sites often link to other sites. You may want to jot down notes about favorite sites. Sometimes you can even print out information that isn't copyright-protected; try the print option and see what happens.

Be prepared: Surfing the Internet can be an addicting habit! There is so much great information. It's a fun way to focus on your future.

#5 SHADOW A PROFESSIONAL

Linking up with someone who is gainfully employed in a profession that you want to explore is a great way to find out what a career is like. Following someone around while they are at work is called "shadowing." Try it!

This process involves three steps.

1. Find someone to shadow. Some suggestions include
   - ☉ the person you interviewed (if you enjoyed talking with them and feel comfortable about asking them to show you around their workplace)
   - ☉ friends and neighbors (you may even be shocked to discover that your parents have interesting jobs)
   - ☉ workers at the chamber of commerce may know of mentoring programs available in your area (it's a popular concept, so most larger areas should have something going on)
   - ☉ someone at your local School-to-Work office, the local Boy Scouts Explorer program director (this is available to girls too!), or your school guidance counselor
2. Make a date. Call and make an appointment. Find out when is the best time for arrival and departure. Make arrangements with a parent or other respected adult to go with you and get there on time.
3. Keep your ears and eyes open. This is one time when it is OK to be nosy. Ask questions. Notice everything that is happening around you. Ask your host to let you try some of the tasks he or she is doing.

The basic idea of the shadowing experience is to put yourself in the other person's shoes and see how they fit. Imagine yourself having a job like this 10 or 15 years down the road. It's a great way to find out if you are suited for a particular line of work.

BE CAREFUL OUT THERE!

Two cautions must accompany this recommendation. First, remember the stranger danger rules of your childhood. NEVER meet with anyone you don't know without your parents' permission and ALWAYS meet in a supervised situation—at the office or with your parents.

Second, be careful not to overdo it. These people are busy earning a living, so respect their time by limiting your contact and coming prepared with valid questions and background information.

PLAN B

If shadowing opportunities are limited where you live, try one of these approaches for learning the ropes from a professional.

Pen pals. Find a mentor who is willing to share information, send interesting materials, or answer specific questions that come up during your search.

Cyber pals. Go on-line in a forum or chatroom related to your profession. You'll be able to chat with professionals from all over the world.

If you want to get some more on-the-job experience, try one of these approaches.

Volunteer to do the dirty work. Volunteer to work for someone who has a job that interests you for a specified period of time. Do anything—filing, errands, emptying trash cans—that puts you in contact with professionals. Notice every tiny detail about the profession. Listen to the lingo they use in the profession. Watch how they perform their jobs on a day-to-day basis.

Be an apprentice. This centuries-old job training method is making a comeback. Find out if you can set up an official on-the-job training program to gain valuable experience.

Ask professional associations about apprenticeship opportunities. Once again, a School-to-Work program can be a great asset. In many areas, they've established some very interesting career training opportunities.

Hire yourself for the job. Maybe you are simply too young to do much in the way of on-the-job training right now. That's OK. Start learning all you can now and you'll be ready to really wow them when the time is right. Make sure you do all the Try It Out activities included for the career(s) you are most interested in. Use those activities as a starting point for creating other projects that will give you a feel for what the job is like.

WHAT'S NEXT?

Have you carefully worked your way through all of the suggested activities? You haven't tried to sneak past anything, have you? This isn't a place for shortcuts. If you've done the activities, you're ready to decide where you stand with each career idea. So what is it? Green light? See page 150. Yellow light? See page 149. Red light? See page 148. Find the spot that best describes your response to what you've discovered about this career idea and plan your next move.

RED LIGHT

So you've decided this career is definitely not for you—hang in there! The process of elimination is an important one. You've learned some valuable career planning skills; use them to explore other ideas. In the meantime, use the following road map to chart a plan to get beyond this "spinning your wheels" point in the process.

Take a variety of classes at school to expose yourself to new ideas and expand the options. Make a list of courses you want to try.

Get involved in clubs and other after-school activities (like 4-H or Boy Scout Explorers) to further develop your interests. Write down some that interest you.

Read all you can find about interesting people and their work. Make a list of people you'd like to learn more about.

Keep at it. Time is on your side. Finding the perfect work for you is worth a little effort. Once you've crossed this hurdle, move on to the next pages and continue mapping out a great future.

YELLOW LIGHT

Proceed with caution. While the idea continues to intrigue you, you may wonder if it's the best choice for you. Your concerns are legitimate (listen to that nagging little voice inside!).

Maybe it's the training requirements that intimidate you. Maybe you have concerns about finding a good job once you complete the training. Maybe you wonder if you have what it takes to do the job.

At this point, it's good to remember that there is often more than one way to get somewhere. Check out all the choices and choose the route that's best for you. Use the following road map to move on down the road in your career planning adventure.

Make two lists. On the first, list the things you like most about the career you are currently investigating. On the second, list the things that are most important to you in a future career. Look for similarities on both lists and focus on careers that emphasize these similar key points.

Current Career	Future Career
☼ _____	☼ _____
☼ _____	☼ _____

What are some career ideas that are similar to the one you have in mind? Find out all you can about them. Go back through the exploration process explained on pages 137 to 146 and repeat some of the exercises that were most valuable.

☼ _____
☼ _____
☼ _____
☼ _____

Visit your school counselor and ask him or her which career assessment tools are available through your school. Use these to find out more about your strengths and interests. List the date, time, and place for any assessment tests you plan to take.

What other adults do you know and respect to whom you can talk about your future? They may have ideas that you've never thought of.

What kinds of part-time jobs, volunteer work, or after-school experiences can you look into that will give you a chance to build your skills and test your abilities? Think about how you can tap into these opportunities.

GREEN LIGHT

Yahoo! You are totally turned on to this career idea and ready to do whatever it takes to make it your life's work. Go for it!

Find out what kinds of classes you need to take now to prepare for this career. List them here.

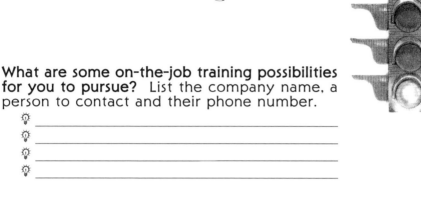

What are some on-the-job training possibilities for you to pursue? List the company name, a person to contact and their phone number.

- _____
- _____
- _____
- _____

Find out if there are any internship or apprenticeship opportunities available in this career field. List contacts and phone numbers.

- _____
- _____
- _____
- _____

What kind of education will you need after you graduate from high school? Describe the options.

- _____
- _____
- _____
- _____

No matter what the educational requirements are, the better your grades are during junior and senior high school, the better your chances for the future.

Take a minute to think about some areas that need improvement in your school work. Write your goals for giving it all you've got here.

- _____
- _____
- _____
- _____

Where can you get the training you'll need? Make a list of colleges, technical schools, or vocational programs. Include addresses so that you can write to request a catalog.

- 💡 _____
- 💡 _____
- 💡 _____
- 💡 _____

HOORAY! YOU DID IT!

This has been quite a trip. If someone tries to tell you that this process is easy, don't believe them. Figuring out what you want to do with the rest of your life is heavy stuff, and it should be. If you don't put some thought (and some sweat and hard work) into the process, you'll get stuck with whatever comes your way.

You may not have things planned to a T. Actually, it's probably better if you don't. You'll change some of your ideas as you grow and experience new things. And, you may find an interesting detour or two along the way. That's OK.

The most important thing about beginning this process now is that you've started to dream. You've discovered that you have some unique talents and abilities to share. You've become aware of some of the ways you can use them to make a living—and, perhaps, make a difference in the world.

Whatever you do, don't lose sight of the hopes and dreams you've discovered. You've got your entire future ahead of you. Use it wisely.

SOME FUTURE DESTINATIONS

Wow! You've really made tracks during this whole process. Now that you've gotten this far, you'll want to keep moving forward to a great future. This section will point you toward some useful resources to help you make a conscientious career choice (that's just the opposite of falling into any old job on a fluke).

IT'S NOT JUST FOR NERDS

The school counselor's office is not just a place where teachers send troublemakers. One of its main purposes is to help students like you make the most of your educational opportunities. Most schools will have a number of useful resources, including career assessment tools (ask about the Self-Directed Search Career Explorer or the COPS Interest Inventory—these are especially useful assessments for people your age). They may also have a stash of books, videos, and other helpful materials.

Make sure no one's looking and sneak into your school counseling office to get some expert advice!

AWESOME INTERNET CAREER RESOURCES

Your parents will be green with envy when they see all the career planning resources you have at your fingertips. Get ready to hear them whine, "But they didn't have all this stuff when I was a kid." Make the most of these cyberspace opportunities.

- ⚘ The Career Center for Teens (a site sponsored by Public Television Outreach) includes activities and information on 21st-century career opportunities. Find it at http://www.pbs.org/jobs/teenindex.html.
- ⚘ Future Scan includes in-depth profiles on a wide variety of career choices and expert advice from their "Guidance Gurus." Check it out at http://www.futurescan.com.
- ⚘ Just for fun visit the Jam!z Knowzone Careers page and chat with other kids about your career dreams. You'll find them by going to http://www.jamz.com and clicking on the KnowZone icon. (Note: This site is monitored!)
- ⚘ JobSmart's Career Guides is another site to explore specific career choices. Look for it at http://www.jobsmart.org/tools/career/spec-car.htm.

IT'S NOT JUST FOR BOYS

Boys and girls alike are encouraged to contact their local version of the Boy Scouts Explorer program. It offers exciting on-the-job training experiences in a variety of professional fields. Look in the white pages of your community phone book for the local Boy Scouts of America program.

MORE CAREER BOOKS
ESPECIALLY FOR SPORTS FANS

To find out more about how to make sports a part of your career plans, consult the following books. They provide information about additional career options for sports fans.

Bonner, Staci. *Now Hiring: Sports.* New York: Crestwood House, 1994

Career Research Monographs. *Careers in Sports Administration.* Chicago: Institute for Research, 1996.

Cylkowski, Greg. *Developing a Lifelong Contract in the Sports Marketplace.* Little Canada, Minn.: Athletic Achievements, 1992.

Field, Shelly. *Career Opportunities in the Sports Industry.* New York: Facts On File, 1991.

Heitzman, W. Ray. *Careers for Sports Nuts and Other Athletic Types.* Lincolnwood, Ill.: VGM Career Horizons, 1991.

———. *Opportunities in Sports and Athletic Careers.* Lincolnwood, Ill.: VGM Career Horizons, 1993.

Kaplan, Andrew. *Careers for Sports Fans.* Brookfield, Conn.: Millbrook Press, 1991.

Nelson, Cordner. *Careers in Pro Sports.* New York: Rosen Publishing Group, 1990.

Taylor, John. *How to Get a Job in Sports.* New York: Macmillan Books, 1992.

HEAVY-DUTY RESOURCES

Career encyclopedias provide general information about a lot of professions and can be a great place to start a career search. Those listed here are easy to use and provide useful information about nearly a zillion different jobs. Look for them in the reference section of your local library.

Cosgrove, Holli, ed. *Career Discovery Encyclopedia: 1997 Edition.* Chicago: J. G. Ferguson Publishing Company, 1997.

Encyclopedia of Career Choices for the 1990's. New York: Perigee Books/Putnam Publishing Group, 1992.

Maze, Marilyn, Donald Mayall, and J. Michael Farr. *The Enhanced Guide for Occupational Exploration: Descriptions for the 2,500 Most Important Jobs.* Indianapolis: JIST, 1991.

VGM's Careers Encyclopedia. Lincolnwood, Ill.: VGM Career Books, 1997.

FINDING PLACES TO WORK

Use resources like these to find leads on local businesses, mentors, job shadowing opportunities, and internships. Later, use these same resources to find a great job!

Kobak, Ed, Jr. *Sports Address Bible.* Santa Monica, Calif.: Global Sports Publishing, 1996.

Latimer, Jon. *Sports Scholarships and College Athletic Programs.* Princeton, N.J.: Peterson's, 1998.

LeCompte, Michelle. *Job Hunter's Sourcebook: Where to Find Employment Leads and Other Job Search Resources.* Detroit: Gale Research Inc., 1996.

Also consult the Job Bank series (Holbrook, Mass.: Adams Media Group). Adams publishes separate guides for Atlanta, Seattle, and many major points in between. Ask your local librarian if they have a guide for the biggest city near you.

FINDING PLACES TO PRACTICE JOB SKILLS

An apprenticeship is an official opportunity to learn a specific profession by working side by side with a skilled professional. As a training method, it's as old as the hills, and it's making a comeback in a big way because people are realizing that doing a job is simply the best way to learn a job.

An internship is an official opportunity to gain work experience (paid or unpaid) in an industry of interest. Interns are more likely to be given entry-level tasks but often have the chance to rub elbows with people in key positions within a company. In comparison to an apprenticeship, which offers very detailed training for a specific job, an internship offers a broader look at a particular kind of work environment.

Both are great ways to learn the ropes and stay one step ahead of the competition. Consider it dress rehearsal for the real thing!

Cantrell, Will. *International Internships and Volunteer Programs.* Oakton, Va.: World Wise Books, 1992.

Guide to Apprenticeship Programs for Non-College Bound Youth. New York: Rosen, 1996.

Hepburn, Diane, ed. *Internships 1997.* Princeton, N.J.: Peterson's, 1997.

Summerfield, Carol J., and Holli Cosgrove. *Ferguson's Guide to Apprenticeship Programs: Traditional and Nontraditional.* Chicago: Ferguson's, 1994.

NO-COLLEGE OCCUPATIONS

Some of you will be relieved to learn that a college degree is not the only route to a satisfying, well-paying career. Whew! If you'd rather skip some of the schooling and get down to work, here are some books you need to consult.

Abrams, Kathleen S. *Guide to Careers Without College*. Danbury, Conn.: Franklin Watts, 1995.

Corwen, Leonard, *College Not Required!: 100 Great Careers That Don't Require a College Degree*. New York: Macmillan, 1995.

Curless, Maura. *Careers Without College: Fitness*. Princeton, N.J.: Peterson's, 1992.

Farr, J. Michael. *America's Top Jobs for People Without College Degrees*. Indianapolis: JIST, 1997.

Jakubiak, J. *Specialty Occupational Outlook: Trade and Technical*. Detroit: Gale Research Inc., 1996.

Richardson, Allan F. *Careers Without College: Sports*. Princeton, N.J.: Peterson's, 1993.

Unger, Harlow G. *But What If I Don't Want to Go to College?: A Guide to Success through Alternative Education*. Rev. ed. New York: Facts On File, 1998.

INDEX

Page numbers in **boldface** indicate main articles. Page numbers in *italics* indicate photographs.

sports information director
105
sports pro 111
sportswriter 117
trainer 123–24

P

party hosting 97–98
personal trainer 49, 109
physical education 30, 49,
110
trainers 121
physical fitness
fitness instructor 48–54
trainer 120–27
physical therapist 49, 50, 53
play-by-play announcers
78, 79
player *See* athlete
playground surface 91, 92, 93
press conferences and
briefings 103
product endorsements 20
professional associations *See*
organizations and associations
professional sports *See also*
sports pro
athlete 26–33
coach 34
facilities manager 46–47
information director 102–4
official 61–62

sports attorney 70–71,
75–76
sportscaster 77–85
sportswriter 114–19
trainer 120–21, 124–27
public address announcer
77–78, 79
public relations
souvenirs as 89
sports information director
102–7

R

radio
sportscaster 77, 79
sports information director
102–3
sportswriter 114
Ratliff, Dick 99–101, *99*
reading suggestions 137–38,
140, 157–58, 159
agent 19, 21
athlete 26, 29–30
coach 34, 37
facilities manager 41
fitness instructor 48
official 55, 58
recreation director 63
sports attorney 70
sportscaster 77, 81, 82
sports equipment manu-
facturer 91, 94